TURKEY'S DEMOCRATIC DECLINE

HEARING

BEFORE THE

SUBCOMMITTEE ON EUROPE, EURASIA, AND EMERGING THREATS

OF THE

COMMITTEE ON FOREIGN AFFAIRS
HOUSE OF REPRESENTATIVES

ONE HUNDRED FOURTEENTH CONGRESS

SECOND SESSION

JULY 13, 2016

Serial No. 114–196

Printed for the use of the Committee on Foreign Affairs

Available via the World Wide Web: http://www.foreignaffairs.house.gov/ or
http://www.gpo.gov/fdsys/

U.S. GOVERNMENT PUBLISHING OFFICE

20–746PDF   WASHINGTON : 2016

For sale by the Superintendent of Documents, U.S. Government Publishing Office
Internet: bookstore.gpo.gov   Phone: toll free (866) 512–1800; DC area (202) 512–1800
Fax: (202) 512–2104   Mail: Stop IDCC, Washington, DC 20402–0001

COMMITTEE ON FOREIGN AFFAIRS

CONTENTS

TURKEY'S DEMOCRATIC DECLINE

WEDNESDAY, JULY 13, 2016

House of Representatives,
Subcommittee on Europe, Eurasia, and Emerging Threats,
Committee on Foreign Affairs,
Washington, DC.

The subcommittee met, pursuant to notice, at 2:54 p.m., in room 2200, Rayburn House Office Building, Hon. Dana Rohrabacher (chairman of the subcommittee) presiding.

Mr. ROHRABACHER. I call the subcommittee to order. This is our second subcommittee event of 2016 focused on the development of the situation in Turkey. And as we continue to watch with concern, I have titled today's hearing, "Turkey's Democratic Decline."

Let me say from the offset that our comments, and even our criticisms, of the Turkish Government are predicated on a deep respect for Turkey and the Turkish people. Turkey and America have been and are friends. Friends speak plainly to one another about problems. That is what you will hear today.

I would like to take this opportunity to extend my condolences to the families of all the victims of last month's terrorist attack at Istanbul's airport. It was a cowardly attack by radical Muslim extremists. And traveling through that region, I was able to personally pay a tribute to the victims of this horrendous massacre just a few days after the tragic event had occurred.

Our expressions reflected those of sorrow, expressed and reflected those of the American people. Turkish victims are no different than American victims. These people have been murdered in recent months and recent years by radical extremists, represent an evil force on this planet that must be defeated and destroyed. And both of our countries, Turkey and the United States, will be a safer people and place when that happens.

Those of you who have observed this subcommittee know, that while wishing the best for Turkey, we have concerns about actions taken by President Erdogan that may put his people at risk and weaken the strong ties between our countries. Our hope for a better situation and things would turn around has not happened, and we have been disappointed. And there is a mounting body of evidence suggesting that President Erdogan's party and his regime seems to be involved with corruption and misrule that is taking Turkey in exactly the wrong direction.

President Erdogan's party has used the levers of power to limit dissent and to crack down on free journalism. Thousands of judges and prosecutors have been reassigned based on their political incli-

(1)

nations. And immunity from parliamentarians have been lifted, opening the way for charges to be used against them in order to sideline opposition, especially those in the HDP.

Seemingly erratic, Erdogan has officially designated the followers of Mr. Gulen as a terrorist group, and this group was once, of course, a lynchpin of his political coalition. So he has gone from a relationship with a group that has been very important to his success to now declaring them as enemies and declaring them the enemies of his country. They helped bring him to power and now he has targeted them for repression.

These kind of steps have taken Turkey further away from the shared values at the heart of our American-Turkish alliance. While a representative from the Committee to Protect Journalists couldn't be here today in person, they did send a written statement, and I will be submitting the entire statement for the record. But I wanted to read a short excerpt from it now.

The Committee to Protect Journalists reports that over the past 2 years the Turkish Government, and I quote,

> "Increased its repressive action against the press through using vague, broadly worded antiterrorist laws, bringing charges under an archaic law that carries jail terms for insulting the President, replacing the editorial management of opposition media outlets and firing their staff, routinely imposing bans on the reporting of sensitive stories, and prosecuting and imprisoning journalists on antistate charges in retaliation for their work."

That is, indeed, a sad description for the state of free media in Turkey. It is a sad description of how Turkey has changed in these last 5 years and has gone in the wrong direction. While I have always strived to maintain a balanced perspective, it is clear to me that Erdogan's actions have hobbled Turkey's democracy at home and left his country more isolated in the region than at any other time in recent memory.

I have many questions for our witnesses today, but I especially look forward to their views on the recent rapprochement between Turkey, Russia, and Israel. While such developments are, of course, welcome, I can't help but wonder if this is merely a momentary change of attitude or something more durable. We can get into that during the testimony.

With that said, I thank our witnesses. And without objection, all members will have at least until the end of this week to submit additional written questions for extraneous material for the record.

I now turn to Mr. Meeks, the ranking member, to have whatever opening statement he would like.

Mr. MEEKS. Thank you, Chairman Rohrabacher. And thank you for your remarks and organizing today's subcommittee hearing on the political trends in Turkey.

As we all know, and as, I guess, clearly indicated even by the number of individuals that is in this room, Turkey is our important ally in an increasingly complex region. And, you know, I am grateful, especially grateful for the opportunity to take a look at Turkey again and again and again because that is how important our relationship is with Turkey.

You know, when I first came into Congress, I looked at the number of countries around and the various regions, Turkey is truly an important ally and a country that I think that we have got to work with. And when you have friends, you should be able to talk honest and open with your friends. You know, it reminds me of some of the dialogue that we have here in the United States currently that is going on around our country and the talk is let's have a dialogue, and dialogue at times has to be frank.

So when we look at some of the trends in Turkey, we see that some remain the same since our last hearing. Domestically President Erdogan continues to enjoy strong support but has not veered from his push toward the presidential system. The domestic conflict with the Kurds has not abated and is closely linked with the conflict in Syria. And as a result of the Syrian war, the refugee crisis in agreement with the EU has also remained a source of strain.

On the other hand, there have been some other changes, some significant. A Prime Minister resigned in May. Terror attacks have struck the cord of fear, detracting tourists from visiting Turkey and further crippling their economy. These attacks test our resolve, our common values in an open society, and tip the balance between liberty and security.

On the international front, Turkey and Israel recently signed a broad agreement to restore ties after a 6-year break, a step that I say that I welcome. Furthermore, Turkey's looking to restore relations with Russia, reopening a needed source of tourism. And yesterday, Prime Minister Yildilrum announced efforts to seek normalization with Syria, possibly presenting new opportunities for peace building and cooperation.

Yet, where does that leave Turkish-U.S. and Turkish-NATO relations? And what can we do in Congress to make sure Turkey remains an ally and a friend and a trusted partner in the region? I believe it begins and ends with our commitment to our common principles and shared interests, and that brings us back to the democratic space in Turkey.

We, in Congress, are indeed concerned with democratic progress in Turkey. I inquire about its state, as a concerned friend, as I said. I want to make sure—it is imperative to discuss the recent crackdown on the freedom of speech in Turkish universities and in the press. Tolerance in the face of domestic criticism is difficult, and regional events further complicate the situation.

But nevertheless, we must fully defend the fight for academic freedom, for freedom of the press, and for the right of individuals to critique their governments, as difficult as that may be to hear. I say that here in the United States for the people of the United States, and I say that there for the people of Turkey, that they must have the freedom to express themselves.

As we all know too well here in America, suppressing these voices only leads to an erosion of democracy, a hollowing out of society, and even an eruption of conflict. And as violence spreads across southeastern Turkey and into beautiful Istanbul, we are reminded of the delicate balance between security and liberty. Tragically, these are not isolated incidents. They serve to highlight the need for a path to peace in Turkey, Iraq, and Syria.

So I too want, as the chairman indicated, send my condolences out to those who suffered losses at the recent attacks at the Turkish airport. We all looked with harrowing eyes as terror attacks took place there, and we wish and hope that the families—I know that they are undergoing tremendous loss and pain, and our prayers go up to them and their families.

So I think that, Mr. Chairman, as I yield back to you, I hope that this hearing helps us to understand and bring a peace that is closer to our reality and help strengthen our relationship while we have some frank conversation and dialogue. I look forward to listening to the witnesses, because your testimony is important to me understanding and learning, and I think that, you know, those who are listening to this hearing, so that we can get information out, we can share and work together.

Because the idea here is, when we have to be critical, let's be critical. But it is not just for the sake of being critical; it is for the sake of trying to make sure that we are all going to have a better tomorrow and better relationships between our countries and we can only do that with honest dialogue.

And I yield back.

Mr. ROHRABACHER. Well said.

Mr. Trott, do you have an opening statement?

Mr. TROTT. I would like to thank the chairman and ranking member for holding this timely and important hearing.

I would also like to thank the witnesses for taking time to be here today.

It seems like every time we try and hold Turkey accountable for their actions, their response is, but we are a NATO ally. Turkey certainly remains one of our allies, but that does not make them immune to honest and fair criticism. Turkey's insouciance to democracy and human rights under President Erdogan is disturbing.

Just a couple days ago, Human Rights Watch reported that the Turkish Government is blocking independent investigations into alleged mass abuses against civilians across southeast Turkey. These abuses include heinous crimes like unlawful killings of civilians and mass force civilian displacement.

I also remain concerned about the seizing of various Armenian churches in Turkey, including Surp Giragos in April. This is reminiscent of the events that led to the Armenian genocide over 100 years ago. And while I am discussing the genocide, I would like to applaud the German Parliament for overwhelmingly adopting a resolution calling the coordinated campaign to exterminate the Armenians in 1915 a genocide.

All of us on this panel are lucky to be able to express our ideas freely and without fear of repercussions. Ordinary citizens and journalists in Turkey, however, do not have this privilege. Turkey remains one of the worst countries in the world when it comes to freedom of the press, and we got to see that firsthand in April when the President came to Brookings and his security repeatedly harassed, assaulted, and even reportedly tried to throw out media that they did not like.

If this is how Erdogan's police act in Washington, one can only imagine how they act in Turkey. Mr. Chairman, Turkey's progress toward democracy is on a downward spiral. They are a country facing a myriad of issues, both domestically and internationally. Continuing down this disturbing path, when they are denying history, expropriating land, and severely restricting freedom of the speech, is not the answer.

I yield back.

Mr. ROHRABACHER. Thank you very much.

Ms. Gabbard, do you have an opening statement?

Let me just note that tomorrow I will be submitting a Sense of the House resolution based on today's testimony and some of the statements that you have heard in working with my colleagues, a Sense of the House resolution expressing concern about the direction of various societal trends and governmental trends in Turkey.

And so today, I would invite my colleagues to, at the end of this hearing, work with me on developing that particular Sense of the House resolution.

Now with that said, I would like to thank our witnesses for joining us today. We have three distinguished witnesses. Dr. Henri Barkey was the director of Middle East Program at the Woodrow Wilson Center here in Washington. Formally, he was a professor at Lehigh—is it Lehigh?—Lehigh University and authored several books on Turkey and Kurdish issues and served as a member of the State Department's policy planning staff.

We have Dr.—I am really bad at names—Fevzi?

Mr. BILGIN. Fevzi.

Mr. ROHRABACHER. And——

Mr. BILGIN. Fevzi Bilgin.

Mr. ROHRABACHER. There it is, okay. And is the founding president of Rethink Institute, a Washington-based think tank. He is an expert in the areas of constitutional and Turkish politics. He received his Ph.D. in political science from the University of Pittsburgh and has taught politics in both the United States and Turkey in addition to being a published author.

And Alan Makovsky, I remember you. Makovsky, I have known that name before. There you go. A senior fellow at the Center for American Progress, a private think tank in Washington, DC. And from 2001 to 2013, he served as the senior professional member of staff here in the House Committee on Foreign Affairs. We were just reflecting on how neither one of us have changed over those 20 years. He helped us cover the Middle East and Turkey when he worked before us, and today he is here to, again, give us advice and some direction as to what our policies should be toward this situation now in Turkey.

Before, of course, he did all this, he directed the Washington's Institute's Turkish research program and was an employee of the State Department.

So we have three expert witnesses. And, Dr. Barkey, I would suggest we start with you. And I would request that, if we could, keep it down to about 5 minutes. All the rest of your statement will be part of the record for people to read, and if you could keep it down to the 5 minutes, we then could have a dialogue once all the witnesses have testified.

Dr. Barkey.

STATEMENT OF HENRI J. BARKEY, PH.D., DIRECTOR, MIDDLE EAST PROGRAM, THE WILSON CENTER

Mr. BARKEY. Thank you, Chairman Rohrabacher, Ranking Member Meeks, and members of the subcommittee. It is an honor to testify today, and I ask that my written testimony be admitted into the record, please.

Mr. ROHRABACHER. Without objection.

Mr. BARKEY. There is no question that when it comes to issues of free speech, due process, individual and civil rights, the situation in Turkey, has deteriorated significantly over the last 3 years. The atmosphere created by the ruling justice and development party and President Erdogan is not conducive to free discussion of ideas, policies, and politics.

What I will try and do is give you essentially in bullet points what has happened and then try to offer you an explanation. First of all, you have all already alluded to the press. The press is under a tremendous pressure. It is a twofold sets of pressures: One is that you see journalists being fired, newspapers being closed, taken over, same thing happening to television stations, as well as social media. That is one aspect of it.

The other aspect is that there is also simultaneously an attempt to build a parallel, if you want, press that is completely subservient to the President and the party. And it is essentially, when you look at that press on a daily basis, as I do, all you see is essentially the legal education of official propaganda, if you want, but most importantly, what you see is that there is no room for any discussion of any opposing ideas in that place.

So the press is under enormous pressure, and it is not surprising that Freedom House has downgraded Turkey's status from partially free to not free, which is actually quite damning for a country that is a member of the NATO alliance.

But the press is not the only one, and this is important to understand. Every institution of civil society in the State is also under attack with an effort to dominate. It is true for business associations. It is true for academia. Thirty-seven academics have been fired so far. But I know a lot of friends of mine who are under investigation, and more will be fired as time goes by, eventually to be replaced with people who are more conducive to the official position.

Similarly, the judiciary is being revamped and to make it much closer to the government. Even individuals are not immune; 1,845 individuals have been charged for insulting the President, some of the penalties are dire. So far nobody has gone to jail. And even former allies of Mr. Erdogan are under the same oppression.

So why is this change? I mean, the interesting thing is that Mr. Erdogan and his party came to power, and in a paradoxical way it was the biggest and most important opening of the Turkish political system ever, since 1923, I would say. They came out against the military, they came out against traditional ruling elites, and for a while they ruled in that way.

But they changed. They changed, I would argue, for two reasons: One is Mr. Erdogan has won victory after victory and he thinks he is invincible, but most importantly, he actually does feel vulnerable. He feels vulnerable because Turkish civil society is still quite dynamic, can resist, can disagree, and, as we saw in elections in 2015, actually defeat Mr. Erdogan. But Mr. Erdogan is the President not the Prime Minister. The Prime Minister has all the legal powers that the constitution gives, so he feels vulnerable in the Presidential powers, so to say.

But fundamentally, I would argue, the real reason for the change is Mr. Erdogan's decision to not make peace with the Kurdish—the PKK and with the Kurds. In fact, he was making enormous progress in that direction, commendable progress. And he scuppered the peace negotiations after his own people had signed the document. And the reason he did it—and this also—we won't have time for this—but explains the changes in foreign policy. The reason he did it is because of the threat it perceives from the Syrian Kurds, in Syria, as the Syrian Kurds, who have aligned themselves with the United States, make progress and move against ISIS.

In the process, what he is afraid of is that a Syrian Kurdish entity that is closely aligned with the Turkish Kurds will emerge and therefore pose a strategic threat to Turkey. And he decided—this is the reason why he decided to essentially go on that rampage against the press, against the Kurds.

And in some ways, it also explains the changes that you see today in foreign policy because, as he finds himself isolated, he is trying to reconfigure his friendships, or so he thinks, with the idea that he will come up with a common, shall we say, cause against the Kurds.

And I will stop here. The red light has gone on.

[The prepared statement of Mr. Barkey follows:]

House Foreign Affairs Subcommittee on Europe, Eurasia, and Emerging Threats
Turkey's Democratic Decline
July 13, 2016
Henri J. Barkey
Director, Middle East Program
Woodrow Wilson Center

Chairman Rohrabacher, Ranking Member Meeks, and members of the subcommittee, it is an honor to testify before you today. I ask that my written testimony be admitted into the record.

There is no question that when it comes to issues of free speech, due process, and individual and civil rights, the situation in Turkey has deteriorated significantly in the last three years. The atmosphere created by the ruling Justice and Development Party (AKP) and President Recep Tayyip Erdoğan is not conducive to free discussion of ideas, policies, and politics. President Erdoğan has been in effect violating the Turkish Constitution by acting in a partisan way, interfering with all institutions of the state and society, from Parliament to parties to the press to municipalities and academia.

What makes this situation paradoxical is that in the beginning of AKP rule in the early 2000s, Erdoğan and his party were in the vanguard of an unprecedented liberalization of social and political space. A bureaucratic-military secular elite that derived a much support from an urban intelligentsia and business elite wedded to the ideas of Turkey's modern founder, Kemal Atatürk, had traditionally governed Turkey.

The AKP opened up the political space and allowed for previously banned or underrepresented voices to have their day in the sun. Still, the Turkish military remained as a powerful force behind the scenes, carefully monitoring AKP's actions always fearful that the party would pursue policies deemed too "Islamic." In 2007, in a critical strategic error, the military high command decided to block AKP stalwart and foreign minister Abdullah Gül's quest to run for the presidency. By throwing caution to the wind, the military allowed the AKP to mount a counter attack. In national elections called by the AKP, where this was the preeminent issue, the electorate delivered a stinging rebuke to the military by reelecting the AKP with a much larger share of the vote.

The defeat of the military liberated the AKP from its only powerful nemesis. The impact of this development would not become evident for some time. The change really emerged after 2013; in his quest to outmaneuver the military and populate his administration with experienced cadres, Erdoğan had made an alliance with Fethullah Gülen, a religious leader with a substantial following and the bête noire of the military. Fearful of the military, Gülen had sought refuge in the United States. That alliance ended when tapes of conversations of the then Prime Minister Erdoğan and others were leaked to the media detailing extraordinary accounts of corruption at the highest levels of the government.

Erdoğan quickly went on the counterattack and began to dismantle the Gülen organization in the state bureaucracy and everywhere else—most importantly in the media. Even before this denouement, Erdoğan had already begun to create his own press establishment. Today, much of the press is controlled directly by surrogates of President Erdoğan or owned by people who are completely subordinate to him by virtue of financial and business deals. The pro-government press and websites are essentially used as tools to intimidate and attack opponents. What is left of the independent press is working under exceedingly difficult conditions with almost no advertising revenue and with limited access to institutions, such as Turkish Airlines that buys papers in bulk. Television stations are being pushed out of the satellite networks that are broadcast everywhere in the country. Many papers, including the Gülen-owned large circulation *Zaman,* have been taken over by the state.[1] Even websites are under danger of being blocked; some 104,904 websites have had access restricted as of April of this year. Social media is often the target of government controls such as shutdowns or slowdowns. At this rate, there will be no independent press to speak off. Even in the

---

[1] When *Zaman* was taken over its archives, some 27 years of materiel, were deleted, thereby robbing everyone, most importantly future researchers, of access to rich data.

days when the military exercised a great deal of control behind the scenes and the political class was quite subservient to the officers' preferences, there was a much livelier press. As a result, Freedom House downgraded Turkey's press status from *partly free* to *not free* in 2013. Today there are an estimated 34 journalists in jail with the most recent arrests only a week ago.[2]

Even the largest independent media group, the Doğan Group, has seen its wings clipped; tax evasion charges levied at the owners have had the effect of the Damocles's Sword. The newsgroup has lost staff—fired or forced to resign—as the group as a whole eschewed its role as custodian of the public good. It started with the 2016 Gezi protests when the Doğan owned CNN-Turk refused to cover the events in Taksim Square live, preferring instead to run a documentary on penguins. Most recently the group's news agency, DHA, simply stated what the government prosecutor alleged when it issued arrest warrants for three journalists working for a pro-Kurdish news agency, DIHA: it, too, claimed without any proof that the three journalists were members of the PKK, the Kurdistan Workers' Party.

The general atmosphere of intimidation has been expanded with the liberal use of libel laws against individuals. Since August 2014, some 1,845 criminal cases have been opened up for insulting the President. Although few such cases end up in the defendant going to jail, the government has relied on this tactic to harass the opposition and its allies and in the process intimidate them. Academia has not been immune from these kinds of pressures. As of June 2016, some 37 academics have fired from both public and private universities, most because they signed on to a petition criticizing the government. It is widely expected that the probe into the 1,000+ academics that signed the petition will continue to claim more and more victims as the police continues to question "suspects."

The origins of the change in Turkish domestic policy on democratic rights can be attributed to two different political developments and interests. The first has to do with

---

[2] European Federation of Journalists, http://europeanjournalists.org/journalists-in-jail-europe/

the return to armed conflict with the PKK after a hiatus of more than two years. The conflict has caused much destruction throughout the southeast as the PKK decided to take the fight to the cities; hundreds of civilians have been killed along with more than 500 members of the security services and an untold number of PKK fighters. To date, large sections of many cities are still under curfew despite the end of hostilities months ago as residents cannot return or even claim their property. A recent report by <u>Human Rights Watch vividly details the attempts by the Turkish state to block independent investigations into alleged mass abuses of civilians.</u>[3]

The ceasefire collapsed primarily because Erdoğan decided to scupper peace negotiations between his representatives and those of the imprisoned PKK leader, Abdullah Öcalan, over disagreements about the future of the Syrian Kurds where the PKK affiliate and U.S. ally, the Democratic Union Party (PYD), has emerged as a critical force. Erdoğan wanted Öcalan and the PKK to halt PYD's advances for fear that an emerging future Syrian Kurdish entity, led by a group allied if not created by the PKK, would strategically threaten Turkey in the long run. When the PKK refused to go along, Erdoğan refused to recognize the "Dolmabahçe" agreement his lieutenants had signed with the Kurdish side. By abandoning the process, he also sought to shore up support among hardliners in society and the military. Most ominous is his decision to give immunity to members of the armed forces fighting the PKK; in effect, they cannot be prosecuted for any violation of individual rights no matter how odious they may be.[4]

The other reason for the regime's hardening stance on freedom of expression has to do with both the Gülen challenge and the resulting corruption revelations and with the need to change the political system from a parliamentary to a presidential system. The corruption revelations and the 2013 mass Gezi protests demonstrated to Erdoğan that he was vulnerable. The vulnerability existed not just among the electorate but also with other institutions of the state, namely the judiciary. If anything, the June 2015 elections demonstrated how real that danger was as his party lost its majority in Parliament. Had

---

[3] Human Rights Watch, "Turkey: State Blocks Probes of Southeast Killings," July 11, 2016.

[4] Reuters, "Turkey grants immunity to security forces fighting militants," June 24, 2016.

it not been for his rapid maneuvering and the dysfunction within the Nationalist Movement Party (MHP) that prevented the formation of an opposition governing coalition that allowed him to turn the tables on his opponents, Erdoğan would have found that his political powers—almost absolute now though not formal—could have been severely curtailed. Hence he singlehandedly forced a second election under heightened tensions and conflict with the PKK that returned the AKP to power.

Erdoğan has extended his control over just about every institution: having purged his original partners from 2002 and replaced them with weak politicians who have no significant base of their own, therefore deriving any legitimacy or power from proximity to him, he now completely controls his party. Similarly, other state institutions are in the process of being revamped to his benefit, these include the bureaucracy, intelligence, and police. The state's judicial system is being revamped. He has created a network of businessmen who are subservient to him; a virtuous cycle of sorts as the beneficiaries of state contracts then enrich the coffers of the ruling party. Academia is also in the process of being transformed either by dismissals or the appointment of university presidents in opposition to faculty-wide election results.

Future Prospects

The prospects are dim. Erdoğan will change policies only when he deems them to be counterproductive as was the case with the negotiations with the PKK or the recent U-turns in foreign policy with Israel, Russia, and potentially with Egypt and even Syria and Iraq. Turkey has become a one-person state. In short, therefore, it is quite possible for him to alter policy but the cost and benefit calculations would have to have changed to force him to do so.

Mr. ROHRABACHER. Dr. Bilgin.

STATEMENT OF FEVZI BILGIN, PH.D., PRESIDENT, RETHINK INSTITUTE

Mr. BILGIN. Chairman Rohrabacher, Ranking Member Meeks, and the members of the committee, thank you for the opportunity to testify before you today on Turkey's democratic decline. And I ask that my full written testimony be admitted into the record.

It is fair to say that all the major political developments in Turkey in the last 5 years can be attributed to Recep Tayyip Erdogan's presidential aspirations. A de facto Turkish-style presidential system is already in place, where Erdogan appoints and dismisses Prime Ministers, shapes the cabinet, packs the court in bureaucracy with sworn loyalists.

The final step is to make a constitutional amendment that will set the new regime in stone. Freedom of speech and freedom of press is under fire. Thousands of journalists were already fired since 2013. There is no mainstream media left, only a few daring but small outlets for dissent. Independent media outlets are seized or censured, and social media is routinely blocked.

An important casualty of the Erdogan's political aspirations and Turkey's democratic decline is the community known as the Gulen or Hizmet movement. The government has targeted the movement especially since the outbreak of the corruption scandal in Turkey in December 2013.

According to Erdogan and his lieutenants, the corruption allegations brought forward were, in fact, an insidious attempt to topple the AKP government. They claim that this was orchestrated by Gulen movement affiliates nested in the judiciary and police forces. The Gulen movement on the other hand has vehemently denied these allegations, calling them baseless accusations serving to cover up the corruption.

The movement essentially is a faith-based network of individuals, organizations, institutions, inspired by the ideas of Turkish-Islamic scholar Fethullah Gulen, who is now residing in the United States. It subscribes to a moderate, Sufi version of Islam, along with emphasis on interfaith dialogue.

In Turkey, the movement established private high schools in every town, mostly which became nationally ranked institutions. Graduates of these schools moved onto both the public and private sectors, many joined the government bureaucracy. The movement also launched influential media outlets in Turkey. The network showed noticeable efficiency, dynamism, defying the traditionally introverted and subdued culture of Turkish conservatism.

However, the movement quickly overreached itself in Turkey. The sheer size of the network exposed it to the ill intentions of those who sought influence and leverage. A penchant for high politics in some circles seemingly undermined the message of tolerance and inclusion that characterizes the larger movement.

The media affiliated with the movement, on the other hand, while promoting democratization, demilitarization of politics, and EU membership, alienated the foes of the AKP government, which in better days was pursuing those very same objectives. The reputation of the movement media was also tainted when they underemphasized the irregularities and misconduct during the coup trials several years ago of military officers, journalists, and academics.

The movement in Turkey now faces blanket persecution. According to the news, state news agency, as of July 2016, more than 4,000 individuals have been detained and about 1,000 have been sent to jail. The detainees are from all walks of life and include businessmen, doctors, teachers, journalists, academics, philanthropists, and even housewives. In addition, the government is taking over privatized schools and colleges, and charity organizations that were established by the movement participants.

Businesses that have financially supported those initiatives are seized on a daily basis. Many have had to flee the country to avoid detention. The remaining hundreds of thousands of individuals that are ordinary citizens dedicated to education, charity, and service, and unrelated to the so-called political struggle are awaiting their fate. The movement-affiliated media has been subjected to a violent and illegal takeover, including the highly circulated ''Zaman'' and ''Bugun'' newspapers, and several TV stations, resulting in the firing of thousands.

As an annual report published by the U.S. Department of State attests, Turkish courts have been going through political pressure in the last few years. As a result, people in the movement, as well as other dissidents, will not have a chance to stand a fair trial, despite very serious accusations leveled against them.

Human Rights Watch stated that the persecutions for membership of an alleged Fethullah Gulen terrorist organization are ongoing, although there is no evidence to date that the Gulen movement has engaged in violence or other activities that could reasonably be described as terrorism. But the lack of evidence of criminal activity did not prevent the government from designating the movement as a terrorist organization. This move allows the government to implement harsher antiterrorism laws for Gulen movement cases.

The Turkish Government also continues to harass the movement outside Turkey. The foreign governments are pressured to shut down schools and other institutions affiliated with the movement in their countries. The Turkish Government has long sought Gulen's extradition to Turkey from the United States. Thus, they launched a litigation campaign against the movements affiliates in the United States, and most recently, a U.S. Federal judge dismissed such a lawsuit in Pennsylvania.

And thank you.

[The prepared statement of Mr. Bilgin follows:]

Testimony before the

U.S. House of Representatives Committee on Foreign Affairs

Subcommittee on Europe, Eurasia, and Emerging Threats

At a Hearing Titled

Turkey's Democratic Decline

by

Fevzi Bilgin, PhD

President

Rethink Institute

Washington D.C.

July 13, 2016

Introduction

Chairman Rohrabacher, Ranking Member Meeks, and members of the subcommittee, thank you for the opportunity to testify before you today on Turkey's democratic decline.

It is fair to say that all the major political developments in Turkey in the last five years can be attributed to Recep Tayyip Erdogan's presidentialist aspirations. In 2014, he succeeded in becoming the first popularly elected president in modern Turkish history, with 52% of the votes. However, the current system is still a parliamentary system, in which, technically speaking, the prime minister runs the country as the executive. Previously as prime minister, and now as president, Erdogan has been leading a very determined campaign, promoting a regime where the president is an elected autocrat with unbridled executive power. A de facto "Turkish-style" presidential system is already in place, where Erdogan appoints and dismisses prime ministers, shapes the cabinet, and packs the courts and bureaucracy with sworn loyalists who are ready to take on political and social dissent, the media and civil society. The final step is to be a constitutional amendment that will set the new regime in stone.

Erdogan has a particular way of doing politics. He dominates the country's agenda. The pro-Erdogan media, whose owners have been financially rewarded by government contracts, disseminates that agenda with similar newspaper headlines and phony talk shows on TV. In fact, Erdogan's iron control of the media is key to understanding his political strategy of augmenting his image and undermining rivals and alternatives even from his own party. The mainstream Turkish media has been under fire, and has been forced to lay off thousands of journalists since 2013. In reality, there is no mainstream media left, only a few daring but small outlets for dissent. Independent media outlets are seized or censured, and social media is routinely blocked.

Turkey is a powerful Muslim nation, a NATO member, and a European Union candidate. Thus, Turkey's actions are very consequential for the immediate region, which is mired in sectarian conflict and is in the midst of the most serious humanitarian crisis in recent history. In the last year, Turkey's battle against ISIS alongside the United States has been overshadowed by the campaign against the Kurdistan Workers' Party (PKK) and its affiliates in Northern Syria. Despite his efforts to obtain international legitimacy, targeting ISIS has had no significant domestic political benefits for Erdogan and the Justice and Development Party (AKP). Despite repeated bombings committed by ISIS in Turkey and the enormous security threats posed by domestic operatives, who allegedly number in the thousands, very few people have been arrested, and no one has been convicted of terrorism.

Persecution of the Gülen Movement

An important casualty of Erdogan's political aspirations and Turkey's democratic decline is the community known as the Gülen (a.k.a. Hizmet) movement in Turkey. The movement has been subjected to political persecution for more than two years by the Turkish government. Erdogan publicly called for a "witch hunt," and arrests, threats, and harassment have now become routine for affiliates and sympathizers of the movement. The government has targeted the movement, especially since the outbreak of the corruption scandal in Turkey. According to Erdogan and his lieutenants, the allegations brought forward by Istanbul prosecutors on December 17, 2013 were in fact an insidious attempt to topple the AKP government orchestrated by Gülen movement affiliates nested in the judiciary and police forces. The Gülen movement has vehemently denied these allegations, calling them baseless accusations serving to cover up the corruption. While the corruption cases were effectively nullified by legislation and executive interventions in the courts, the attacks on the Gülen movement have continued in full force.[1]

The Gülen movement is a faith-based network of individuals, organizations and institutions inspired by the ideas of Turkish Islamic scholar Fethullah Gülen, who is now residing in the United States. It subscribes to a moderate, Sufi version of Islam, along with emphasis on interfaith dialogue, which is considered to be an antidote to radicalism. The movement is known for its vast network of schools, dialogue and cultural centers, and charity organizations. The movement originated in Turkey in the 1970s and has increasingly become international. However, Turkey has always remained at the core of the network. In Turkey, the movement established high schools in every town, most of which became nationally ranked institutions. Graduates of these schools moved on to both the public and private sectors. Many joined the government bureaucracy. The movement also established influential media outlets in Turkey that included the largest daily newspaper and several TV and radio stations. Businessmen sympathizing with the movement established nationwide chambers of commerce that actively sought new markets around the world. The network showed noticeable efficiency, a cosmopolitan spirit despite its faith-based origins, and astounding dynamism, defying the traditionally introverted and subdued culture of Turkish conservatism.

However, the movement quickly overreached itself in Turkey. The sheer size of the network exposed it to the ill intentions of those who sought influence and leverage. Some appeared to have a false sense of power. A penchant for high politics in some circles seemingly undermined the message of tolerance and inclusion that characterizes the larger movement. The movement media has been, and still is, an ardent supporter of democratization, demilitarization of politics, and European Union membership; however, this has sometimes alienated the foes of the AKP government, which in better days was pursuing those very same objectives. The reputation and impartiality of the media affiliated with the Gülen movement were tainted when they underemphasized irregularities and misconduct during the coup trials of military officers, journalists, and academics. For this reason, political and ideological critics of the AKP government also turned against the Gülen movement. Before the recent clash, the movement media had been accused of "carrying the water" for Erdogan.

The clash between the AKP government and the Gülen movement was initially portrayed as a "power struggle," "a tug of war." This was true to the extent that the movement was believed to have considerable political influence in Turkey. The truth actually mirrored what had happened to all of Erdogan's former allies, liberals and democrats, some of whom were among the AKP founders: They were taken advantage of in the process of consolidating power. Following the corruption scandal, the AKP government quickly passed a series of laws in the guise of fighting the "parallel structure" in the state that essentially revoked

---

[1] Reza Zarrab, a Turkish-Iranian trader and the central figure in the corruption scandal in Turkey, was arrested in March 2016 in the United States for conspiring to evade U.S. sanctions against Iran, money laundering and fraud. The case, which corroborates December 17 allegations that Zarrab had paid bribes to ministers for his operations, continues as of this writing: U.S. v. Reza Zarrab, 15-cr-867, U.S. District Court, Southern District of New York (Manhattan).

separation of powers, suspended the rule of law, and restricted the rights and freedoms of everyone. In the end, both pro- and anti-Gülen people filled the very same prison for daring to dissent and question authority.

The Gülen movement in Turkey now faces blanket persecution. According to the state news agency (AA), as of July 2016, as many as 4,444 individuals have been detained; 982 have been sent to jail, and the rest released on probation. Just in the month of June, 433 individuals were detained and 160 were sent to jail. The detainees are from all walks of life and include businessmen, doctors, teachers, journalists, academics, philanthropists and even housewives. In addition, the government is taking over private high schools, colleges, and charity organizations that were established by movement participants. Businesses that have financially supported those initiatives are seized on a daily basis. Many have had to flee the country to avoid detention. The remaining hundreds of thousands of individuals – ordinary citizens dedicated to education, charity, and service and unrelated to the so-called "power struggle" – are awaiting their fate. The movement-affiliated media has been subjected to a "violent and illegal takeover"[2], including the highly circulated *Zaman* and *Bugun* newspapers and several TV stations, resulting in the firing of thousands.

A Judicial Travesty

An annual report recently published by the U.S. Department of State, *Country Reports on Human Rights Practices for 2015 (Turkey)*, vividly describes how the Turkish courts had to bow to political pressure:[3]

> The law provides for an independent judiciary, but the judiciary remained subject to government influence, particularly from the executive branch. Judges who ruled against prosecuting high-level members of the ruling Justice and Development Party (AKP) on corruption charges in 2014 were subsequently promoted to more senior positions, while prosecutors and one judge who had conducted the initial investigation into allegations of corruption were indicted during the year.[4]

As a result, people in the Gülen movement and other dissidents do not have a chance to get a fair trial, despite very serious accusations leveled against them:

> Legal professionals reported that peace courts created legal confusion due to unclear hierarchy and authority. The courts in December 2014, for example, ordered the arrest of Samanyolu Broadcasting Company CEO Hidayet Karaca and other members of the media as well as 33 police officers with alleged ties to Fethullah Gülen, a Muslim cleric accused of operating a clandestine network within the executive and judicial branches with a goal of overthrowing the government. After a higher-level court ruled on April 26 that detainees should be released, the Istanbul chief public prosecutor stated the higher court's decision was null and void because another peace court had simultaneously ruled for the continuation of

[2] *European Parliament Resolution on the 2015 Report on Turkey* (April 2016)
[http://www.europarl.europa.eu/sides/getDoc.do?pubRef=-//EP//TEXT+TA+P8-TA-2016-0133+0+DOC+XML+V0//EN]
[3] *Country Reports on Human Rights Practices for 2015 (Turkey)*, U.S. Department of State (April 2016)
[http://www.state.gov/documents/organization/253121.pdf]
[4] Ibid. p. 16

their detention. The defendants were indicted on September 17, and the case continued at year's end.[5]

Despite the widespread incrimination efforts by government officials and pro-government media, no indictments have been brought so far against the Gülen movement due to lack of credible evidence.

> Prosecutions of journalists, judges, prosecutors, and police for membership of an alleged "Fethullah Gülen Terrorist Organization" were ongoing at time of writing, although there is no evidence to date that the Gülen movement has engaged in violence or other activities that could reasonably be described as terrorism.[6]

> The AKP government in 2015 continued efforts to purge the police and judiciary of alleged supporters of the Gülen movement. During 2015, prosecutors, judges, and police officers with perceived links to the Gülen movement were jailed and charged with plotting against the government and membership of a terrorist organization. The main evidence being cited against judges and prosecutors at time of writing was decisions taken in the course of their professional duties rather than any evidence of criminal activity.[7]

But lack of evidence of criminal activity did not prevent the government from designating the Gülen movement as a terrorist organization that is trying to overthrow the government. This move allows the government to implement harsher antiterrorism laws for Gülen movement cases:

> The HRA asserted there were hundreds of political prisoners from across the political spectrum, including journalists, political party officials, academics, and students. The government stated that these individuals were charged with being members of, or assisting, terrorist organizations...Authorities also used the antiterror laws during the year to detain individuals and seize assets, including media companies, of individuals alleged to be associated with the Gülen movement, designated by the government during the year as the Fethullah Gülen Terrorist Organization.[8]

Antiterrorism laws are used to detain Gülen movement individuals and seize their assets. Regular donations to Gülen movement nonprofits and charity groups are considered to be financing a terrorist group. Consequently, ordinary citizens are arrested for supporting these organizations.

The Turkish government continues to harass the Gülen movement outside Turkey. Foreign governments are pressured to shut down schools and other institutions affiliated with the movement in their countries. The Turkish government also launched a litigation campaign against movement affiliates in the United States. Most recently, a U.S. federal judge dismissed a lawsuit alleging that Fethullah Gülen orchestrated human rights abuses in Turkey, ruling that the plaintiffs "offer only circumstantial and tenuous allegations of a connection between Gülen's domestic conduct and the violations of plaintiffs' rights in Turkey".[9]

---

[5] Ibid. p.17
[6] *World Report 2016*, Human Rights Watch (2015)
[https://www.hrw.org/sites/default/files/world_report_download/wr2016_web.pdf], p. 581
[7] Ibid. p. 582
[8] U.S. Department of State, p. 19-20
[9] Bunyamin Ates et al v. Muhammed Fethullah Gülen et al, 15-cv-02354, U.S. District Court, Middle District of Pennsylvania.

Conclusion

Turkey's democracy has never been perfect, but it has been a bright spot in the Middle East. However, recent years have seen a substantial decline in democratic institutions, the rule of law, freedom of the press, and freedom of speech, and increasing intolerance toward dissent. One casualty of the deteriorating political climate is the Gülen movement, a faith-based network. Once an ardent supporter of Erdogan's democratization and EU-oriented agenda, the movement has now been outlawed and subjected to blanket persecution. The fate of the Gülen movement is a harbinger of things to come for all who dare to dissent in this new political environment.

Thank you.

Mr. ROHRABACHER. You are next.

STATEMENT OF MR. ALAN MAKOVSKY, SENIOR FELLOW, CENTER FOR AMERICAN PROGRESS

Mr. MAKOVSKY. Thank you, Mr. Chairman.

Mr. Chairman, Mr. Ranking Member, members of the subcommittee, it is an honor for me to testify before you today. As you said in your introduction, I worked here for 12 years as a staffer, from 2001 to 2013. And knowing the——

Mr. MEEKS. Is your mike on?

Mr. MAKOVSKY. Oh, I am sorry. Now it is.

Mr. ROHRABACHER. You should have known that more than anybody.

Mr. MAKOVSKY. I have never been on this side of the table before, sir. I was always a quiet staffer in the background.

Mr. ROHRABACHER. Go ahead Alan.

Mr. MAKOVSKY. Anyway, I just wanted to say that as a former staffer and knowing the great importance accorded hearings such as these, I am deeply privileged to have been invited to testify and I thank you.

I respectfully request that my written testimony, as submitted, be entered into the record.

And I would like to join you, Mr. Chairman, in the condolences you offered to the Turkish people on the June 28 attack on the Ataturk Airport.

The title of this hearing, "Turkey's Democratic Decline," sets out the problem: Turkey's democracy, never as good as it should have been, is indeed rapidly deteriorating. On virtually every front, media, judiciary, political governance, Kurdish rights, private business, universities, as my colleagues here have all detailed, freedom is diminishing and power is being concentrated in President Erdogan's hands. Arguably not since the death of Turkey's founder, Mustafa Kemal Ataturk, and certainly not since the advent of free elections in Turkey in 1950, has one man held so much power in the Turkish system.

President Erdogan's primary focus, perhaps more correctly his obsession these days, is to formalize a Presidency-based system in Turkey in place of the longstanding parliamentary system. His second and third-ranking priorities, probably in that order, are ridding Turkey of any Gulenist influence, real or imagined, and defeating the PKK and, related to that, quashing any Kurdish movement for collective rights.

Certainly, because of the horrific terrorism staged by ISIS over the past year in Turkey, I have no doubt that fighting ISIS has also become more of a priority for Turkey, and Turkish officials now speak of the importance of fighting ISIS and the PKK simultaneously. But I don't believe that President Erdogan yet sees ISIS as quite as serious a threat to his power and to Turkey as he sees the Gulenists and the PKK.

I know there is already a lot of overlap in this testimony, and I don't want to do another catalogue of all the human rights abuses. Let me throw out, on freedom of the press, yet another NGO's report. Reporters Without Borders, in its 2016 World Press Freedom Index, actually ranks Turkey just 151st out of 180 countries—three slots behind Russia, by the way. So it is not a positive record. Another study has said that 70 percent of the Turkish print media, and a similar portion of the electronic media, is now a mouthpiece of the government, either owned directly or slavishly supportive of the government.

I know my time is rapidly diminishing here, so maybe—look, you know, I would like to say a little more about what is going on with the Kurds. I think——

Mr. ROHRABACHER. You have time. Please do.

Mr. MAKOVSKY. Ranking Member Meeks, you very specifically in the last hearing in February—you talked about the importance of dialogue today and you analogized it to the civil rights movement in this country, which I am certainly old enough to remember and to have been a small part of.

Look, I think what is going on—the assault on the Kurds in the southeast is a terrible mistake. The PKK is not blameless. It was a mistake for them to declare autonomy in various zones, to goad the Turks. It was a mistake for them to build up their weapons during the ceasefire.

But the response of the Turkish military, I think, has really caused tremendous destruction, dislocation that at one point created several hundred thousand displaced persons within Turkey. That fact got very little publicity. And we saw some of the pictures, such as from Cizre that reminded us of pictures from Kobani. Again, I don't think the PKK is blameless, but I think the approach that Turkey has taken is completely wrong and has alienated the Kurdish population and made it more difficult to enter into that dialogue that you spoke about.

In my written testimony, I speak a bit about what the future should be of U.S.-Turkish relations. And I don't have time—I don't know if I have time to just quickly list a couple of the principles, but——

Mr. ROHRABACHER. We will get it in the questions. There you go.

Mr. MAKOVSKY. Okay. I will be happy to end it there. Thank you very much.

[The prepared statement of Mr. Makovsky follows:]

TESTIMONY OF ALAN O. MAKOVSKY
SENIOR FELLOW, CENTER FOR AMERICAN PROGRESS
HOUSE COMMITTEE ON FOREIGN AFFAIRS,
SUBCOMMITTEE ON EUROPE, EURASIA, AND EMERGING
THREATS
HEARING: TURKEY'S DEMOCRATIC DECLINE
JULY 13, 2016

Chairman Rohrabacher, Ranking Member Meeks, Members of
the Subcommittee:

It is an honor for me to testify before you today. Having
worked as staff on the Foreign Affairs Committee from 2001 to
2013, and knowing the importance accorded hearings such as
these, I feel particularly privileged to return to this hearing
room as a witness.

The title of this hearing, "Turkey's Democratic Decline," sets
out the problem: Turkey's democracy, never as good as it
should have been, is indeed rapidly deteriorating. On virtually
every front – media, judiciary, political governance, and
Kurdish rights – freedom is diminishing and power is
becoming concentrated in President Erdogan's hands.
Arguably not since the death of Turkey's founder, Mustafa

Kemal Ataturk – and certainly not since the advent of free elections in Turkey in 1950 -- has one man held so much power in the Turkish system.

President Erdogan's primary focus is to formalize a Presidency-based system in Turkey in place of the long-standing Parliamentary system. His second- and third-ranking priorities, probably in this order, are ridding Turkey of any Gulenist influence (real or imagined) and defeating the PKK and, related to that, quashing any Kurdish movement for collective rights.

Regarding the Presidency, as he hasn't detailed a proposal yet, the precise nature of the Presidential system he envisions remains unclear – whether it's to be American-style, French-style, or, as many suspect, Putin-style. He has made clear, however, that he considers checks and balances to be a nuisance that holds back Turkey's progress.

None of these goals promotes strong adherence to freedom of thought or expression. In fact, they are playing out in just the opposite manner. In its 2016 World Press Freedom Index,

Reporters Without Borders ranks Turkey 151st out of 180 countries, three slots behind Russia.

In President Erdogan's drive to impose his point of view, he has succeeded in dramatically limiting the reach and impact of opposition or even neutral media. He has done this in a variety of ways. In some cases, he has intimidated ownership through manipulation of the tax system, sometimes succeeding in forcing unfriendly publications out of business, while arranging their purchase by his supporters.

Reporters and other writers face constant intimidation. Notwithstanding Turkey's constitutional guarantees of freedom of the press and its formal adherence to the Universal Declaration of Human Rights, writers know that they can be prosecuted for insulting the President if they are too critical of Erdogan's policies or even for supporting terrorism if they are too critical of the government's policies regarding the Kurds. Or, they can simply be fired if their writings bring their newspaper into confrontation with the government. Or –- and this is probably the most common occurrence – they can simply be told by their superiors to tone down their writings or avoid certain topics so as to avert problems.

In the case of the closure of the Gulenist-associated *Zaman*, which was said to be Turkey's mostly widely circulated newspaper, the government simply took over the paper on the spurious claim that it was being financed by "terrorists," obviously meaning Gulenists. It has done likewise with other Gulenist-associated media.

I think it's worth noting that, until the closure of *Zaman*, that newspaper – along with mass-appeal *Hurriyet* and low-circulation but strongly secularist *Cumhuriyet* – were seen as the three most significant non-government dailies. Over the past year, the editors-in-chief of all three have been prosecuted for what most of the democratic world would see as merely exercising their journalistic duties.

To be sure, there are still critical voices – primarily in the print media – but most of these are individuals who have succeeded in establishing reputations or connections in the West. However, even such reputations or connections are no guarantee of job protection; I'd wager everyone who works on

Turkish issues in Washington knows at least a couple of prominent Turkish journalists who have either been prosecuted or lost their jobs because they were too critical of the government.

Regarding the crime of "insulting the President," I should note that this is based on article 299 of the Turkish penal code. It is applied broadly, not only to writers and political cartoonists but also to ordinary citizens, including a 16-year-old boy who was arrested for calling Erdogan a "thief" during a political demonstration.

Article 299 has been on the books since the early days of the Turkish Republic in the 1920s, but no President seems to have applied it as broadly as Erdogan. According to one NGO's research, Erdogan's predecessor President Abdullah Gul applied it 139 times during his seven-year term and Gul's predecessor, President Necdet Sezer, applied it 26 times during his seven-year term. Even 26 times seems 26 times too much in a democracy, but, comparatively, it is a paltry amount compared with its usage during the Erdogan Presidency. According to Turkey's own justice ministry, as of March 1 of this year – that is, over the first eighteen months of the Erdogan Presidency – 1,845 prosecutions had been pursued on the insult charges. That means that, over that period of time, Erdogan was being insulted to the point of legal action a little more than three times a day.

As press freedom recedes and pro-government media dominates, an unfortunate by-product is the wide berth given to anti-American and anti-Western scapegoating. For example, two days after the horrible June 28 terrorist attack that murdered 44 people at Istanbul's Ataturk Airport, one prominent pro-government newspaper headline claimed that the perpetrator was the CIA – even as the Turkish government itself was blaming ISIS. How to explain this divergence? Theoretically, it could be that the government and the newspaper simply came to different conclusions, based on an honest assessment of the facts. It seems far more likely, however, that the government was trying to have it both ways, a sober assessment internationally and a populist, anti-U.S. assessment for its political base.

Turkey has always been rife with stories of U.S.-backed conspiracies, but that is more true than ever in recent times – a product, in my view, of President Erdogan's and the government's not infrequent resort to emotional and questionable charges leveled against the U.S. and the West. For example, on November 27, 2014, Erdogan told a standing committee of the Organization of Islamic Cooperation, meeting in Istanbul, that Westerners "look like friends, but they want us [Muslims] dead; they like seeing our children die." Such an attitude helps explain repeated surveys in recent years showing the U.S. with high unfavorability ratings in Turkey.

Limits on democracy in Turkey are not confined to freedom of expression. A recent law in Turkey has greatly tightened Erdogan's control of the judiciary. Another gives the government the right to expropriate private businesses – yet another the right to expropriate private universities. Those laws are perhaps mainly aimed at rooting Gulenists out of the judiciary, impoverishing Gulenist businessmen and thereby the movement as a whole, and denying Gulenists independent intellectual centers. However, their potential application is far broader and seemingly can be extended to non-Gulenists as well.

One more point regarding the Gulenists: Turkey's recent designation of the movement as a terrorist group is absurd. I have my own criticisms of the Gulenists, but I've never seen the slightest shred of credible evidence linking them to violence or violent intent.

Turkey also recently passed a constitutional amendment that lifts long-standing parliamentary immunity, at least for the current parliament. As a result, it seems likely that 52 of the 59 parliamentarians from the Kurdish-movement-linked Peoples' Democracy Party (HDP, by its Turkish acronym) will be prosecuted for alleged links to the PKK and, once convicted, removed from Parliament. This has been coupled with other forms of pressure on Kurdish political activists, including the arrest of numerous mayors elected from HDP's local affiliate in Turkey's Kurdish-populated southeast and including the very leader of that party. And, of course, Turkey's heavy military response to PKK provocations in the southeast have further angered the local population, at least some meaningful portion of which initially blamed the PKK for the renewal of clashes.

Taken together, these actions form another blow to forlorn hopes of reviving efforts at a peaceful, negotiated solution to the Kurdish question in Turkey.

One common thread in Erdogan's furious reaction to both the Gulenists and the Kurds: In both cases, he seems to feel spurned by those whose loyalty he feels he has earned.

U.S.-Turkish relations: Looking forward

Mr Chairman, all of us on this panel likely agree that Turkish democracy has regressed in recent years. The question is what, if anything, the United States can do about it. And, indeed, that is a thorny question. Turkey has considerable leverage in the bilateral relationship. At times, we may have more; at times, they may have more.

Turkey has always been, first and foremost, an ally valued for its strategic location. The more pressing our need for access to Turkish bases -- most famously, Incirlik Air Force Base -- the greater Turkey's leverage in our bilateral relationship. And, of course, when we're fighting a war, as we are now against ISIS, that need for access is quite pressing.

During the Cold War, which gave birth to the U.S.-Turkish alliance, Turkey had NATO's longest common border with the Soviet Union. Shortly after the Cold War, then-Assistant Secretary of State for European Affairs Richard Holbrooke declared Turkey "the new front-line state," asserting that it is "at the crossroads of almost every issue of importance to the United States on the Eurasian continent."

And that is the manner in which it is primarily viewed even today. Access to Turkey's Incirlik Air Force Base in southern Turkey, hard won through nearly year-long negotiations, is critical to our war on ISIS.

It can be tempting, therefore, not to say much publicly about Turkey's democratic shortcomings, out of concern that Ankara's response will be to deny us access. It is important to do our best not to give in to that temptation, lest we appear cynical about our own central values and lest we dispirit those who look to us for support on legitimate issues of freedom. At the same time, when we criticize, we should criticize as a friend, not as an antagonist. That is the spirit in which my testimony is offered today.

I would not claim that the balance is easily struck between pursuit of strategic interests in Turkey and support for human rights in Turkey.

For example, the European Union -- once the most vocal proponent of human-rights reform in Turkey -- has been largely silenced in that regard over the past several months because of its need for Turkish cooperation on the refugee issue.

We need to be resolute regarding support for Turkey's security against external threats. It was a mistake for us and other NATO partners to withdraw our Patriots from southern Turkey last fall, just as the Russian build-up in Syria was underway. My understanding is that Turkish officials would also welcome more U.S. naval port visits in the Mediterranean at this time of Russian build-up in that strategic arena.

We should be supportive in principle, as we already are, of Turkey's right to defend itself against the PKK. The PKK is on our terrorist list because it kills civilians. That does not mean, however, that we should not speak out against use of excessive force and collective punishment. The Turkish assault on several cities and towns in its southeast – however much it may have been provoked by needless PKK declarations of autonomy – created mass suffering, widespread dislocation, considerable destruction, and, no doubt, deep alienation that will only complicate Turkey's relations with its Kurdish population in the future.

We should speak out strongly against abuses of freedom of the press and politically-motivated arrests in Turkey. At a time when Turkey is regrettably under assault from so many directions, we should remember that Turkey still needs the U.S. and the Western Alliance and will not cavalierly weaken security ties because we speak out. I should note that both President Obama and Vice-President Biden have made important gestures regarding human rights in Turkey this year. Turkey may not do everything we suggest, but they will hear what we say and, at least at times, take it into account.

We should also strongly support the right of Kurds to cultural freedom and democratic expression. That means speaking out about Turkish government efforts to quash the Kurdish movement by criminalizing freedom of speech, removing the

Kurdish presence in parliament, and by using excessive force that amounts to collective punishment.

I believe the U.S.-Turkish relationship will endure because both parties continue to need each other – reinforced by the important NATO link that serves Turkish interests in many ways beyond simply strengthening bilateral relations with Washington -- and so we likely will continue to muddle through. That said, it is hard to deny that both serious policy disagreements and a more negative tone have increasingly infused bilateral relations in recent years.

Accordingly, it behooves our policy-makers to consider whether there might be other regional alternatives that would lessen our dependence on Turkish assets in the years ahead. I don't know if that is being done, but I would hope so.

Thank you, Mr. Chairman.

Mr. ROHRABACHER. All right. My first question is, what were you just going to say?

Mr. MAKOVSKY. Well, first and foremost, Turkey has always been an ally valued for its strategic location, which has been the center-piece of our bilateral relationship. The more pressing our need for access to Turkish bases, most famously Incirlik Air Force Base, the greater Turkey's leverage in our bilateral relationship.

And of course, when we are fighting a war, as we are now against ISIS, that need for access is quite pressing. It can be tempting therefore not to say much publicly about Turkey's demo-cratic shortcomings out of concern that Ankara's response will be to deny us access.

It is important to do our best not to give in to that temptation, lest we appear cynical about our own values, lest we de-spirit those many Turks who look to us for support on legitimate issues of free-dom. At the same time, when we criticize, we should criticize as a friend, as you said, Mr. Chairman, not as an antagonist.

Perhaps we might think of the following principles: First of all, we should be fully supportive of Turkey regarding external threats. I think it was a mistake for us to withdraw Patriots from southern Turkey last fall just as the Russian buildup in Syria was starting. I think we should make more port visits in the Mediterranean, as I have heard requested from Turkish officials.

Second of all, we should be supportive in principle, as we already are, of Turkey's right to defend itself against the PKK, which is on our terrorism list because it has killed civilians.

But the Turkish assault on several cities and towns in its south-east, as I said, has created mass suffering and deep alienation that only complicates Turkey's relations with its Kurdish population now and in the future. We should speak out strongly against abuses of freedom of the press and politically motivated arrests in Turkey. I know President Obama and Vice President Biden have made important gestures in that regard this year.

And thirdly, we should also strongly support the right of the Kurds to cultural freedom and democratic expression. That means speaking out about all Turkish Government efforts to quash the Kurdish movement by criminalizing freedom of speech, removing the Kurdish presence in Parliament, again, as we have heard al-ready, and by using excessive force that amounts to collective pun-ishment.

If I could, Mr. Chairman, just quickly add, I do think we have to prepare for a better day also. I know that NDI and IRI have some important freedom-supporting programs in Turkey, and I think it is important that those be supported.

Mr. ROHRABACHER. We will note that. And I think that it is al-ways important for us when we are dealing with a country that has been so close to us, and such a friend, that whenever there are some very noticeable areas of conflict where we disagree now and we are not operating, that we make sure we do our very best to confront those issues in a way that will facilitate more friendship rather than driving a country away. And that is hopefully what we are doing today.

Where does the panel come down on this, the fact that Turkey now has apologized to Russia on shooting down the plane? Let me just note that I was horrified that they shot the plane down in the first place, and now they are apologizing for it. What is that all about? And what is all this about where we have—Turkey has made very, how do you say, hostile moves toward Israel in the last few years and now it seems to be reaching out to go the opposite direction. What is the take of the panel on those two things, Doctor?

Mr. BARKEY. Well, first of all, I would say that in the Russia case it was very clear that they had made a huge mistake and they had paid a very big price economically with the collapse of tourism. Tourism collapsed because of the violence and the terrorism but also because of the Russians.

The deal with Israel is actually more interesting. I don't think it is a real warming up of relations. It is more cosmetic. But fundamentally, it is not about improving diplomatic relations but it is about gas. Eventually, the Turks want—and the Israelis also very much are pushing for a gas pipeline from the Israeli gas fields, which will go through Cyprus and then to Europe. And, in fact, there is a way in which this is a good sign, because that means that maybe the Cyprus is—there will be a deal in Cyprus, that we will be moving toward a Cyprus settlement.

But the unfortunate aspect of this is that this charm offensive has, especially with Syria now, has another downside. It has a major downside to it. And it is possible that he is—Erdogan is going to double down on the PYD in Syria and on the PKK in Turkey in a way in which he—Erdogan sees the PYD as essentially the most important threat to Turkey, because he thinks because the PYD is a creation of the PKK, that you will have essentially a front, a Kurdish front.

Paradoxically, the Turks, who used to be very opposed to the KRG, to the Iraqi Kurdish movement, are now very close to it. They could have done the same thing with the PYD. The PYD was looking to establish relationship with the Turks. But for Erdogan, he made a strategic decision, and all this charm offensive now, all this moving on, I fear, is for a doubling down on the anti-PYD policy.

And I think that is going to be problematic for us given the fact that we have now a relatively robust alliance with the PYD in fighting against ISIS. And that is the thing we need to watch, I think, much more carefully than anything else which have immediate repercussions.

Mr. ROHRABACHER. My time is used up now, and we will have a second round.

Mr. Meeks.

Mr. MEEKS. Thank you, Mr. Chairman.

Thank you for your testimony.

And I just want to see if I can get some further understanding domestically what is going. And you are right, as I was trying to identify in the past, talking about some of the lessons learned from us in the United States and what has taken place, it is the prism from which I work.

So for example, when someone tells me that the Turks are trying to pack the court, I don't get too upset at that because we are trying to pack the courts here also, you know. That has been the big issue here, who is going to win this election so that the Supreme Court—it makes a difference. So that I am not upset about.

But I am upset about when there are journalists and others who want to express what their views are and that they are incarcerated as a result of that. And/or when there is the big debate, which my question is now, that is taking place about constitutional reform process of which I am not clear on.

So I know that there is some renewed talks about the constitutional reform process. I know it took place there prior, in 2012, and things broke down. So my question is, where are we now, and what is at stake in regards to this dialogue internally in the prospects for greater instability internally in Turkey, and how will that affect us as an ally?

Mr. BILGIN. Well, let me just interject here. The constitutional reform is an important aspect of the last really several years of Turkish politics, as I mentioned, that it has all started with Erdogan's presidential aspirations. Technically, nobody understands why presidentialism is needed in Turkey.

But the first attempt to reform constitution in 2012 collapsed because of that interjection of presidentialism as an AKP proposal. And, now after that, several other elections that AKP and Erdogan won and now it is on the table again. And what is being demanded or what is being aimed is to build a regime, which is called presidential regime, but in actuality it is a one-man rule where, you know, somebody will be an elected autocrat with unbridled executive power. That is what it will end up with, and that is why it is very controversial.

So the system is parliamentary system at the moment. And normally, as we heard before, the Prime Minister is the executive, chief executive of the government. But there was just a switch of Prime Ministers last month, and everybody forgot about that already, I think, because everybody knows who is pulling the threads.

And people are afraid, are concerned that, you know, as Erdogan—as powerful as he is now, how is he going to be when he is an elected President with all these powers. So that is a major concern. And the timeline goes, either we need a constitutional amendment in the Parliament or a referendum.

Mr. MEEKS. Let me just ask then maybe, Mr. Barkey, given that—could there be—if, you know, there is talk about a constitutional reform process, you know, could it be a fair election or not? I mean, I have recently just seen what took place in the U.K, whether they are going to, you know, stay into the EU or not. But that seemed to be an open and a fair election.

So are you saying that there cannot be an open and fair expression of the people of Turkey, that it will be so weighted down because of the heavy handedness of Mr. Erdogan that it won't be transparent and clear? Is that——

Mr. BARKEY. Look, in Turkey, historically, elections have been clean and people have enormous amount of trust in the electoral process. But for the first time now, that faith in the electoral system is disappearing very quickly, and it is clear now that you will not get fair elections anymore. There are enough people who are now saying that the system is rigged.

The AKP gets enormous amount of money from contributions from businesses that get funneled so that it can use for elective purposes. The difficulty with press is completely controlled now. [Microphone off.] You have 70 percent of that being even higher, but by the government and its allies, therefore you cannot have free elections or should we say fair elections. Free elections, yes, but fair elections, which is really contrary to—since 1950 a process of free and fair elections.

Mr. MEEKS. My last question on this round then would be, would you say that is the fact that the outside, what is going on in Syria, what is going on with the PKK, what is going on with the PYD, does that have an effect domestically also on whether or not the Turkish people allow, you know—well, the authoritarian policies to increase that it seems to be happening now in regards to Mr. Erdogan?

Mr. BARKEY. Well, unquestionably. Whenever you have—you can pose the PKK, the Kurdish threat as an alien threat, and that allows you to clamp down obviously on freedom of speech; therefore, that affects the elections, I mean, by definition. And if you go to the southeast, I mean, in the Kurdish areas, you have this amazing military presence, you have this amazing oppression that you see.

So yes, I mean, the notion of—plus people have been displaced, 500,000 people have been displaced. When are they going to vote? How are they going to vote? Are they going to be able to vote? What happens to the Syrian refugees? Will they be able to vote? I mean, there is all these things now going on that has undermined people's confidence in the electoral process.

Mr. MEEKS. I have a question for you in the next round.

Mr. ROHRABACHER. Mr. Trott.

Mr. TROTT. Thank you, Chairman.

My questions are to the entire panel, and anyone can feel free to opine. I wonder if anyone could give me insight into what the status of the Armenian churches that were seized by the Turkish Government and what the status of the churches are at this point.

Mr. MAKOVSKY. Congressman, the only one that I am personally familiar with—maybe my colleagues know more—is the one that is located in the Sur district of Diyarbakir. Right now the whole district is essentially closed, so no one can have access to the church, including worshipers.

Mr. TROTT. Okay. Thank you.

With respect to the Muslim brotherhood, so they have been shunned by much of the Middle East, but the President has chosen to embrace them and is still controlling channels on television. What is the reason behind that, and why shouldn't we be concerned by that?

Mr. BILGIN. The Muslim brothers, there was a support for Muslim brothers, it was a part of a general policy of the Turkey's Middle East policy to basically support these opposition elements that kind of seem a little—look like AKP. And now, as you said, some Equfan elements were residing in Turkey. And now it seems that Turkey's ready to make a shift again, making a peace with General Sisi so that it is likely that they will be kicked out soon, I mean, of Turkey.

Mr. BARKEY. I don't think ideologically that Mr. Erdogan has changed his mind about the Muslim brotherhood. I think he is very sympathetic to them. He is very quick on his feet. I mean, he changes policies when those policies don't work for him, and clearly he has decided now a rapprochement with Egypt and with Israel, given that Hamas is also part of the brotherhood is convenient for him.

But I would say that fundamentally, in terms of where his loyalties and where his preferences lie, they are with the Muslim brotherhood. So what you will see is probably policies of dissimulation other than real change when it comes to this issue.

Mr. MAKOVSKY. Just as a historical matter, when the Sisi takeover happened, it was in the middle of major demonstrations going on in Turkey. I think it brought out Erdogan's paranoia, both in terms of his fear that something immediate from these demonstrations might happen and also based on Turkey's history. I think he has always been concerned about the possibility of a military coup.

And so I think that is what it reflected. But I do agree with Henri that I don't think we are likely to see him change his spots anytime soon. And I am skeptical that things will move forward on relations with Egypt anytime soon. His foreign minister has talked about it, but Erdogan made some very strong anti-Sisi statements after the foreign minister spoke.

Mr. TROTT. Thank you.

And then lastly, with respect to Turkey's priorities in Syria, and how do they align with the United States and where do they diverge generally?

Mr. BARKEY. Well, they have—at the beginning, we were on the same page. We both thought that Assad would leave in 6 months. When that failed and when the opposition failed to come up with serious resistance to Assad, you saw Turkey's support for Jabhat al-Nusra increase. And this came to a boil in 2013 when President Erdogan visited the White House. He was confronted with that. He was asked to stop supporting Jabhat al-Nusra.

The problem is that in the process of supporting Jabhat al-Nusra, a major infrastructure of jihadist supporters was created in Turkey, who funneled people and arms to Jabhat al-Nusra with government support but also people who went to ISIS.

But where we are now today, for us, priority number one is ISIS; for Erdogan it is the PYD then Assad, and then ISIS. So in that sense, in there, we are not on the same page. For him, both the PYD and Assad, even though he is talking about overtures to Assad, are far more important and far more than the jihadist threat.

Mr. MAKOVSKY. Just to elaborate a bit, I agree on the divergences. His primary focus is the Syrian Kurds and Assad. Ours is defeating ISIS. He wouldn't mind if ISIS is defeated in the process, but it is not his priority.

Second of all, and I think it is the number one issue in U.S.-Turkish relations right now, is the fact that we are working closely with the YPG, with the Syrian Kurds, which he considers part of the PKK. And indeed, he has some reason to see their origins in the PKK. And from his point of view, it is U.S. support for a terrorism group.

And, as I say, I noticed in a respected Turkish polling company survey this month, Metropoll, 73 percent of Turks said that the U.S. sides with terrorists against Turkey. It is a very disturbing kind of answer, but I am certain that what it is about is this disagreement about the YPG.

Mr. BILGIN. Yeah. Congressman, despite repeated bombings committed by ISIS in Turkey, an enormous threat that is posed by the domestic operatives, which may number to like in thousands, so far very few ISIS members were arrested and no one has been convicted out of terrorism or something so far. So this is kind of unbelievable basically, given the fact that, you know, Turkey has been bombed like one after another, latest in Istanbul Airport. Maybe Istanbul Airport may change the situation.

Mr. TROTT. Thank you very much.

Mr. ROHRABACHER. All right. And now Ms. Gabbard.

Ms. GABBARD. Thank you, Mr. Chairman.

Mr. Makovsky, your last comment about the poll is interesting, because as we look at Dr. Barkey's comments about Turkey arming and directly aiding al-Nusra, which is an al-Qaeda affiliate, this goes to the crux of the question of our relationship with Turkey, as our number one priority is, and should be, defeating ISIS, al-Qaeda, and these other jihadist groups. Turkey is directly and has indirectly been supporting them now for years.

So, you know, each of you in your opening remarks spoke about Turkey's democratic shortcomings, lack of freedom of the press, lack of due process, freedom of speech, individual and civil rights violations. We saw last year how the election went and really how the process was manipulated to benefit Erdogan.

We see a direct contradiction in Syria with Erdogan's continued fixation on getting rid of Assad, bombing the Kurds who have been without dispute our most loyal, dependable partners on the ground fighting against ISIS. Turkey's actions have directly strengthened groups like ISIS, al-Qaeda, and al-Nusra.

The question is, you know, Turkey is a NATO partner and they claim to be an ally. When you look at all of these issues, both with democratic values as well as objectives that are directly counterproductive to ours and threaten our security, how can you make the argument for NATO—for Turkey to maintain its status as an ally?

And the follow-up to that is, do you see the current government—do you see a path forward for Turkey being capable of or even interested in changing their policy so that they can actually truly be an ally and a partner?

Mr. BARKEY. This is the $64,000 question. It depends a little bit on the position we take in U.S. Government. Look, I spent time in U.S. Government and I follow U.S. policy carefully. We tend to always shy away of pushing very hard with the Turks.

Because we are always afraid that because we have so many issues on a daily basis, Turkish and American bureaucrats talk on 1,000 different issues. We are very close allies, and there is a constituency for this alliance in Turkey.

But the problem, I think, is that before Erdogan and with Erdogan, we have very early stood our line. Let me just say, look at Putin. Not that I want to place Putin here. But he stood his ground with Erdogan and Erdogan had to essentially capitulate. It reminds me what an Arab diplomat told me in Iraq, this year, he said, we hate what Putin does, but we love the way he does it.

Ms. GABBARD. Can I just ask you a follow-up. You said we have very rarely, if ever, stood our ground against Turkey.

Mr. BARKEY. Right.

Ms. GABBARD. What is this source of this great fear that would cause the United States of America to cower in fear and not standing our ground?

Mr. BARKEY. Look, there is always the basis. There is the NATO relationship. There is the ability of—I mean, we are too integrated with Turkey. And in general, the bureaucracy is very much afraid.

The decision to support the Kurds, in Syria, at the time of Kobani, was taken by the President against the position of his— the State Department and the White House allies—aides, right. They were saying, oh, the Turks will be very upset. He did it. And look at the benefits because the Turks were not opening the bases to the U.S. until then. Once they realized that we were aligning ourselves with the YPG, suddenly they opened the bases.

So there is a way in which we can send Erdogan a message. Look, if Turkey is an ally, even if Erdogan is problematic, even if there are lots of people in Turkey—but at the core, this is a long-term relationship which we have not known how to manage well.

Mr. MAKOVSKY. I think the reason for U.S. reticence is because Turkey is such a strategic ally, because of its location.

Mr. ROHRABACHER. Is your mike on?

Mr. MAKOVSKY. It is.

I think we have been concerned that if we speak out, that we will lose access to important assets like Incirlik Air Force Base. And I think that is what has inhibited us. Just the same way the EU, which used to be the strongest advocate of human rights in Turkey, has largely been silenced because of its concern about the refugee issue and Turkey's ability to manipulate that.

I think we have been, over the years, concerned about Turkey's ability to manipulate our access to what is, after all, its sovereign territory, Incirlik Air Force Base and other facilities. I think we do have to consider—I hope this is going on somewhere in the government—whether there are other assets in the region that at least over the long term could be employed in the way that Incirlik is now, almost solely is in Turkey, and so that we could lessen our dependence on Turkey.

You asked will they change? I don't think that is the trend. I think the trend is toward greater independence, partly because if you look at the whole history of our alliance with Turkey, it has been one of growing Turkish independence. They started off as a very impoverished Third World country and now they are an upper middle income country, as classified by the World Bank. So there has been a normal trend whatever the government.

Second of all, you have a government which is right now—which is very critical of us, and of the West, and has shown very anti U.S. reflexes. I don't think we are going to get—I don't think we are going to see any change under this government.

Mr. ROHRABACHER. Mr. Weber.

Mr. WEBER. Thank you. Mr. Chairman, can we turn the air-conditioner down or on? Apparently this is a hot topic. Gosh, where do we start? Mr. Makovsky.

Mr. MAKOVSKY. It is fine. Alan would be sufficient.

Mr. WEBER. You don't care what we call you, just call you for dinner.

So you said something about the Syrian—his main concern—Erdogan's, was the Syrian Kurds, was it ISIL or Assad you said?

Mr. MARKOLSKY. Erdogan's main concern?

Mr. WEBER. Correct.

Mr. MARKOLSKY. Erdogan's main concern right now is the Syrian Kurdish movement.

Mr. WEBER. Okay.

Mr. MAKOVSKY. But closely related to that, it is getting rid of Assad.

Mr. WEBER. It is Assad.

Mr. MAKOVSKY. Assad, yeah. And that is really—the Syrian Kurdish problem is something new, but our divergence over whether it should be Assad or ISIL as a priority has been going now for several years.

Mr. WEBER. Okay. And I came in late, so some of this may be redundant. Forgive me. One of you said, and I think it was you that said a respectable poling institution in Turkey was Metropoll?

Mr. MAKOVSKY. Yes.

Mr. WEBER. Give me the results of that poll again.

Mr. MAKOVSKY. Yes, they asked—I am getting this approximately right, in the fight with terrorism, who do Western countries like the U.S. and Germany side with, Turkey or the terrorists? And 73 percent said——

Mr. WEBER. This was in Turkey?

Mr. MAKOVSKY. Yes.

Mr. WEBER. Inside Turkey?

Mr. MAKOVSKY. Yes. Seventy-three percent said the West side with the terrorists.

Mr. WEBER. So much of I am reading is about how he has done away with opponents, starting with Fethullah Gulen and the press, and he has, you know, put a lot of them in prison. He just seems to oppress everybody who disagrees with him. How does this polling organization get to apply its trade about him with them under his thumb?

Mr. MAKOVSKY. Well, I think there are still pockets of independent expression in Turkey. As far as I am aware, these polls are done independently. I could see why you might think from that question that it was manipulated, but if you went through the whole survey you might not think that.

Mr. WEBER. Okay. So, so far you don't believe that they are under his thumb?

Mr. MAKOVSKY. This particular polling company? Look, I don't think so because they called the 2015 elections essentially correctly. I think they have shown themselves over the years to be essentially——

Mr. WEBER. Okay. Over how many years?

Mr. MAKOVSKY. Well, they have been at it that I have been aware of for at least, I think, a dozen years.

Mr. WEBER. He has let them continue even in that length of time?

Mr. MAKOVSKY. Yes. I mean people say different things about these polling companies whether they are closer to or further from the regime. People do not currently say that this polling company is close to the regime.

Mr. WEBER. Okay. Okay, fair enough. I think you said in your comments one of you did, I have been reading through the comments that he probably more closely wanted a Putin style system.

Mr. MAKOVSKY. That was me.

Mr. WEBER. That was you, okay. And then you also said I think it was Dr. Barkey that Turkey has been busy, or maybe it was in response to my colleague down on the left, from Hawaii, that Turkey has been arming al-Nusrah.

Mr. BARKEY. Was.

Mr. WEBER. When did that stop?

Mr. BARKEY. It is not completely clear. I mean we asked them in 2013 to stop, but it took a while for them to stop. But it is a lot of informal networks that are independent of the government that still continue to support both al-Nusrah and ISIS. I mean when you think of the bombing in Istanbul the other day, it could not have happen if they did not have domestic help.

Mr. WEBER. Right.

Mr. BARKEY. But that is not the government. That is networks that were created at some time, at some point with the government.

Mr. WEBER. But if the government turns a blind eye he is so busy after the news stations and the people like the Gulen and others, then those who are perpetrating this kind of violence kind of run amok, doesn't they?

This is a question for all three of you really, are there any other countries that you know of NATO, EU or in the United Nations, who you see this kind of power grab going on in any other country? Power grab, in other words, where they are shutting down the press, they are dealing with all the dissidents, they are——

Mr. BARKEY. Unfortunately the list is quite long.

Mr. WEBER. Okay. Nothing in the list is quite long of people or countries?

Mr. BARKEY. Countries. I mean, of leaders in countries where you see this.

Mr. WEBER. You see this same kind of action that you see from Erdogan in other countries. Name one.

Mr. BARKEY. Hungary.

Mr. WEBER. Hungary. There is one. Name two.

Mr. BILGEN. Venezuela during Chavez.

Mr. WEBER. Venezuela, okay. Don't miss my question. In the EU, in the U.N. or in—NATO, EU or U.N., any of those countries?

Mr. BARKEY. U.N. includes everybody so you can go Zimbabwe, you can go Ethiopia. There is a whole series of countries. You are not going to run out of countries.

Mr. WEBER. This level of corruption you would equate those?

Mr. BARKEY. Yes.

Mr. WEBER. That is interesting.

Mr. BILGEN. There is rising trend of authoritarianism in the world at the moment too. So that means Turkey is part of that, it extends even to Hungary, which is part of the European Union.

Mr. WEBER. So you all's testimony today is that you don't put Turkey at the top of that. You can equate those with other countries.

Mr. MAKOVSKY. I think, Congressman, if I could——

Mr. WEBER. Yes, this is a question for all three.

Mr. MAKOVSKY. I think that the Reporters Without Borders ranking that I mentioned is very useful in that regard. There is no other NATO or EU country listed below Turkey. They listed them 151st out of the 180——

Mr. WEBER. Yeah, three behind Russia. I came in late so I didn't hear you testimony.

Mr. MAKOVSKY. That is correct, three behind Russia.

Mr. WEBER. Three behind Russia

Mr. MAKOVSKY. Yes.

I am not an expert on Hungary and no doubt I have read enough about it to know though there are some authoritarian trends going on there, but in Turkey I think it has reached very severe proportions, particularly recently with new laws that will increase his power over the judiciary and possibly over private enterprise as well.

Mr. WEBER. Okay. And Mr. Chairman, I am out of time. If you are in a hurry I have one other question.

Mr. ROHRABACHER. Go right ahead.

Mr. WEBER. Actually, I have three other questions, since you opened the door. He was easy, wasn't he?

So there was a 16-year-old in one of your notes, a 16-year-old boy, who called him a criminal or something? A 15-year-old boy?

Mr. MAKOVSKY. A thief, 16.

Mr. WEBER. A 16-year-old called Erdogan a thief and he wound up in jail. What is his status?

Mr. MAKOVSKY. He was released. If I recall correctly, he was never—it never actually came to trial, but I believe he was held in jail for 4 days.

Mr. WEBER. Are the two of you aware of that case?

Mr. MAKOVSKY. Yes. Am I right, 4 days?

Mr. BILGEN. Yes.

Mr. BARKEY. I don't know that case. I know——

Mr. WEBER. You don't know that case. So from what you heard Mr. Makovsky say is that a travesty?

Mr. BARKEY. Oh, yes. I mean 1,825 people have been prosecuted for insulting the President.

Mr. WEBER. Eighteen-hundred forty-five—now I also read a quote where who was it, Erdogan said to the Organization of Islamic Cooperation meeting in Istanbul, and you may have quoted this Mr. Makovsky so forgive me if it is redundant, he said that Westerners ''Look like friends but they want us,'' speaking about Muslims, ''dead. They like seeing our children die.'' Is that on video?

Mr. MAKOVSKY. That is a good question. I have not seen it. I read it in the Turkish press, in both Turkish and English. The English quote that I used came from the Turkish press—the English-language Turkish press. But I don't know whether it's on video or not.

Mr. WEBER. And does——

Mr. MAKOVSKY. Could I add?

Mr. WEBER. Yes, sir.

Mr. MAKOVSKY. On the issue of the article 299 which criminalizes insulting the Presidency, I thought maybe, if I could, just quickly give you a little context. That is not an Erdogan creation. That has been there since the 1920s. That law has been forever in the books, but it does seem that Erdogan has used it far more frequently than any other President. And just as a point of comparison—and this is based on another NGO study—his predecessor used it 139 times. His predecessor save one, 26 times. He has been using it an average of over three times a day, through March 1st. That 1,845 figure was through March 1st and that is the Turkish Government figure.

Mr. WEBER. Thank you very much for your answer.

Mr. Chairman I yield back.

Mr. ROHRABACHER. All right. It is th intent of the chair to have a sound round. And I will proceed.

And let me just note so far, and what we came into this room understanding, there seems to be a very negative trend going on in Turkey. We have tried we had several hearings, trying our best to reach out and try to let the people of Turkey know, the Government of Turkey know that the United States and the people of United States are grateful for the friendship that they have shown and really are grateful for the role that Turkey has played over the last several decades. However, that trend is very easy to see. There is a cycle of tyranny and a cycle of radicalization that seems to be going on in Turkey that is frightening about where that could lead.

Take a look at what has happened in Pakistan, another country that is strategically located, a friend of ours in the cold war, and what has happened in Pakistan? You have a vicious radicalization with various elements in their society in which you have terrorists—a home base for terrorism, not only in their own country where they are repressing their people with radical Islamists, but also engaging in terrorist acts that might even be traced to the Istanbul airport for all we know, because they have been immersed in this.

But yet trying to reach out—we still give aid to Pakistan, even though they are doing this stuff. So I do not believe that what was happening in Turkey is going to lead to a dramatic departure of our relations, but it might evolve into something that is a nightmare like as what has happened in Pakistan and our relations today.

Let me ask this question of the panel, does anyone on the panel have any information about, or believe, that Turkey was involved with taking weapons from Libya and sending them to Syria? Does anyone on the panel know anything about that? I am just probing here.

Mr. MAKOVSKY. I have heard that charge made, but I——

Mr. ROHRABACHER. All right. But nobody has direct information about it?

Let me just note that there are other—it would be a disaster for us to lose Turkey as a military partner, but there are other countries around that have air bases in that region. I mean Erbil itself could serve as a base for military operations so that Kuwait and any number of countries right there could provide what now is provided by Turkey. What would be bad is to make sure the dynamics that are created by such a large country with significant resources and people going in the wrong direction.

So with that, let me ask this, and one of the things that I find just—it is hard for me to understand this but it has happened in other countries as well, and that is when you have the President of this country, but now the permanent Prime Minister, now the President whatever you want to call him, his whole political base was established with a Gulen movement. Am I pronouncing it right Gulen?

Mr. MAKOVSKY. Gulen.

Mr. ROHRABACHER. The Gulen movement. And as far as I can see and I have studied what they believe and I have talked to some people in that movement, they tend to be people who have high values and are looking for a more open and you say tolerant Islam. That would be very admirable type of—by the way, it would be the equivalent of the Rotary Club in the United States. In essential you have a philosophy of helping other people who also are politically involved and involved in the community efforts to help people.

How is it that the Gulen movement now has been declared public enemy number one by the man who they were actually helped put into power, and over the years has been one of the chief sources of support. How did that come about?

Mr. BARKEY. I would like to say something about the Gulen movement. I mean the Gulen movement, I agree with you, has an image of tolerant Islam. Yes they were allied with Erdogan. When Erdogan came to power he did not have the personnel and it was the Gulen movement that staffed it.

But the Gulen movement also, if you ask the Kurds, the Gulen movement was very hard on the Kurds, because Gulenist judges and prosecutors unleashed lots and lots of cases against Kurds that are still continuing today. There are people who went to prison for nothing. I just met with one of the most important lawyers in the Diyarbakir, a few weeks ago, he spent 4½ years in jail. You know why? Because he was at the demonstration, somebody 5,000 people behind him opened a flag, a PKK flag and the judges and the prosecutors said, oh, you are a member of the PKK because you were standing in front of 5,000 people ahead of you.

Mr. ROHRABACHER. So is that the Gulen movement? Or is that——

Mr. BARKEY. If you go and ask the Kurds, the Gulenists were very, very hard on the Kurdish nationalist movement. There were many ways it was very good. They brought in very good staff, but on one issue they whether very, very hard. So it is not a completely—we have to also acknowledge what was wrong with them.

The reason he turned on them is because he thinks—probably he may be right, that the Gulenists actually exposed the corruption. I mean the people who leaked those tapes off Erdogan and the money issues he thinks are Gulenists.

And today the irony of course is that when he came to power and he aligned himself with Gulen against the military, today it is he and the military against Gulen so the alliances have changed, but——

Mr. ROHRABACHER. So the Gulen movement it ended up exposing some of the corruption——

Mr. BARKEY. Right. That is what he thinks.

Mr. ROHRABACHER [continuing]. That was part of his entourage?

Mr. BILGEN. And it should be added that, we are talking about quite a large network, or it was large, in Turkey. It was influential especially media for some one of the things that I would like to mention is, now that the Cihan news agency, was seized by the government, we don't have a watchdog to actually follow the election. That was the only one, that was the only one.

Now you are going to go learn the election results from state news agency, whatever number they put up it will be the number. But it was always checked against Cihan news numbers before. Since it is a large network, as I said it has—because of that it has usual shortcomings like it's a diverse network, there are nationalists, there are more biased, less biased people, there are more secular, less secular. And there are people who are just minding their business about, like, teaching, opening schools and so on and there are others who are more interested in politics. Right? So it is hard to define where it ends, where it begins, and how a judge or prosecutor is basically considered a part of it while they themselves are rejected and so on.

So there are all these shortcomings and I think nobody can really solve that. And even the movement itself the spokespeople and so on, cannot really address some of these questions.

So in the larger picture especially outside Turkey or something the movement is known by more like dialogue activities, education activities or something. And that seems to be the core of the movement and movement message rather than what happened in the last few years in Turkey in the political scene.

Mr. ROHRABACHER. Go right ahead. Comment on that——

Mr. MAKOVSKY. Let me say two good things about the movement and raise one questionable thing.

First of all I have never seen a shred of evidence that they support anything other than peace. So the declaration of the Turkish Government that the Gulenists are a terrorist group is absurd.

Second of all, in their schools they have taught science and mathematics; they have really emphasized what we would think of as more traditionally secular subjects like science and math. I can't vouch for exactly how they are taught, but I don't know of too many Islamic movements in the world that emphasize science and math. That is a real plus.

Where I think the failing has been and, again, this is not proveable, but I think many followers of Gulen, many Gulenists acknowledge that a significant minority of the police and of the judiciary were Gulenists because they wanted to be part of those organizations and exercise power.

And I think there is evidence, circumstantial evidence, that they did act corporately sometimes and particularly in the anti military

49

trials that went from 2008 through 2011 with manufactured evidence and——

Mr. ROHRABACHER. It seemed to me from just a distance the Gulenist movement is somewhat like the Masons were in our country's history back in the founding of our country, they were idealistic people who had an idealistic philosophy. And again, somewhere between the masons an the Rotary Club. And I think——

Mr. BILGEN. With schools.

Mr. ROHRABACHER. Just one last note here about Turkey and— I will have a closing 1-minute statement.

Mr. Meeks.

Mr. MEEKS. Thank you, Mr. Chairman.

This good conversation and as I am listening I am just thinking in my head that things are always complicated. And I always try to tell my children sometimes, as we are right now, with what is going on in America, trying to look at something from somebody else's point of view, turn it around.

And as I have said in my initial statement, I am really concerned when I see the human rights groups and others denying individuals the opportunity to talk, et cetera. At the same time I understand that some of the interests that the Turks may have is different than what our interest is, because they are in that region and we are not. I also understand the Turks not necessarily just doing exactly what we tell them because it is just in our interest and them not seeing it being in their interest, just as I don't expect someone to tell us to do what is in their interest, if it is not in our interest.

So that happens between countries at times. And so when I listen to the difficulty to the Turks, we talk about the PKK, there, to them they are Daesh. That is their number one terrorist group, not to us, because they are not to us, but to us it is those folks in Syria and Iran who—I call them Daesh because I don't call them an Islamic State they are not an Islamic—they don't practice Islam if you talk to any Muslim.

So there are conflicting interests that are natural. And so I can't see a head of state of a country saying we are going to forget our national interests to go with someone else's. So our difficulty is is trying to figure out how we can bring it together so that both of our interests are taken care of.

So what am I asking? And I go through this with another country all the time. And maybe Mr. Makovsky, we have this dialogue with the chairman all the time.

The other big country that you have got conflicts right now is Russia. And Russia has different interests than we do, Russia though similar to Turkey had an individual that was the Prime Minister that decided he wanted to be the President and all the power shifted. Russia is not with us, we are not with them when they went into the U.K.

So the first question is what is the difference, if there is any, because I am trying to figure out both these countries, between Russia and Turkey?

Mr. MAKOVSKY. Simply put, Turkey is an ally, Russia isn't. Turkey is part of the NATO alliance and that alliance is supposed to be dedicated to freedom and democracy, a key—a core of that alliance. Russia is not part of that. If you separate that fact and look at the trends inside those two countries, they become more similar. And I do—Mr. Erdogan has not spelled out exactly what kind of Presidency he has in mind, but I do worry. Many people suspect that President Putin is his model.

And so you are right if you look at strictly domestic trends: There are a lot of similarities. But if you look at our responsibility, and this is my humble opinion, Mr. Ranking Member, if you look at our responsibility to speak out, it is much greater when we are talking about an ally than when we are not.

Mr. MEEKS. Anybody differ?

Mr. BILGEN. Well, I would like to say that when we look at the larger picture, the political system of Turkey and the people, the public opinion which may be manipulated, but is very much, kind of embedded in Western alliance, NATO in European Union. These are hard facts, these are difficult to change even for a strong person as you are gone as he is now.

So there are two ways to look at this. Some time when I follow the developments in Turkey I just see symptoms of state tradition in Turkey. State tradition in Turkey, is a very powerful tradition which was never democratic through addition. It was always bureaucratic, always prioritize state over the individual. So that has been going on for hundreds of years. It is not going to change quickly as far as I see.

But we can see the anomaly at the moment we are facing as a phase in Turkey's political advancement or we may see it as a breaking point. It didn't break yet, okay but it may break. I think, you know, these next couple of years are critical.

Mr. MEEKS. Let me just ask you this then. So what I am trying to get at is there a way just like our priority is to make sure we get rid of Daesh, now is it such a priority for the Turks that the PKK doesn't exist? And just as we want to get rid of Daesh they went to get rid of PKK. They are saying based upon—that is what I am hearing, based upon the poll that you had, they are saying, well, we want you United States to help us get rid of the PKK because they are terrorizing us. And so how do we—and so there is a balance back and forth as opposed to they are saying, okay, we are allies, but we need you to help get rid of our terrorists.

Now, I am hearing at another point that we need to push back so we should side with some of those folks that might be against them to shut them up a little bit. Where do we get to a balance?

Mr. BARKEY. On the PKK issue, I mean, remember the difference between Daesh and PKK is in the case of the PKK there is an original sin. The original sin is that you had a Kurdish problem in Turkey that was unacknowledged, repressed, very, very violently over the years nobody talked about it, we never talked about it until the PKK emerged and made it essentially an issue. And this by the way is something that Erdogan recognized. After he sat down—he had his government sit down with the PKK leader who was in prison on an island in Turkey and they negotiated a deal. So he decided to renege on the deal, and we have been his allies in the sense that we have been fighting and helping him on the PKK issue and we continue to do so. He essentially reneged on the deal.

It is not like Daesh in the sense that he made a deal, he could have gone ahead and finished the deal and we would not be talking about these problems now. He made his own decision, fair enough. That is where I say we should be able to push back and maybe help maybe being an intermediary we can push back. The important thing to understand about Turkey though—from the tone of the hearing, look this is a country that is very divided at the moment, and it is a country where you still have despite all the pressure, a civil society that is pushing back and fighting back those are our allies.

Mr. MEEKS. All countries are very divided. The United States are very divided.

Mr. BARKEY. I know. But what I am saying to you is the impression we are getting here is the Erdogan has complete control. And I am saying he doesn't have complete control yet. So the fact of the matter is we don't have a substitute, Kuwait and Erbil are not a substitute, Congressman Rohrabacher to Turkey.

I mean Turkey's embedded in NATO. Nobody else is going to replace Turkey from that perspective. We have allies in Turkey that we can work with even if Erdogan is problematic. But we need to hold to our principles and to our policies when we deal with Erdogan.

Mr. MEEKS. Similar to we should do in Russia? These are two big countries that we can't ignore.

Mr. BARKEY. Absolutely. Absolutely.

Mr. MEEKS. We can't ignore Russia, we can't ignore Turkey.

Mr. BARKEY. Right. That is my point.

Mr. MAKOVSKY. The balance is very difficult but you are absolutely right, it has to be a cornerstone principle of ours that we oppose the use of violence for political end so we are correct——

Mr. MEEKS. Absolutely.

Mr. MAKOVSKY [continuing]. To oppose the PKK in that regard. But I think we do have to acknowledge that Erdogan at first—at first—Erdogan came around to negotiating with the PKK indirectly, but almost directly, and he seemed to be the one that reneged on the deal. That doesn't justify the PKK use of violence, not at all. But I think that context is very important.

And, maybe if I could add, why did he renege on the deal? In my view, the emergence of a Kurdish political party that opposed his Presidency plans, I think infuriated him. Just like he felt spurned by the Gulenists, he felt spurned by the Kurds who he felt had reason to be grateful to him and in fact made some very important gains under him.

I visited Diyarbakir several times last year, but I had not been there for 15 years until then, and—this was before the fighting broke out, on my first visit—the gains were immense. He felt they owed him gratitude. I think when the party emerged that, contrary to his expectations, opposed his Presidency ideas rather than supported it, he decided to unleash the furies.

Mr. ROHRABACHER. Well thank you very much. And I would like to thank the witnesses, I just have a very short observation which is of course the prerogative of the chair.

Mr. MEEKS. Of the chair.

Mr. ROHRABACHER. Would you like to have a final word?

Mr. MEEKS. Again just thanking you, very insightful and I thank the chair for having us here. I think in the next few months we should have another one and hopefully in January when I am the chair we will have another one.

Mr. ROHRABACHER. I will be the ranking member, what?

Mr. MEEKS. But I just want to thank you very much. This kind of dialogue is tremendously important for us to air out for us to think about as you move forward. This stuff is not easy, it is not simple, it is complicated. And as many people as I talk to about— one side they are on one side or the other, very similar to here in the United States. If you come and went to one particular State the United States is all one way and talk to someone else and say oh, no, it is another way. And this kind of dialogue is very helpful.

So Mr. Chairman, I think that this commitment to the committee and hearing is very timely and very important to looking at what we are doing on the Foreign Affairs Committee as far as foreign policy.

Mr. ROHRABACHER. Yes. I think Mr. Meeks and I have a very good relationship and I think it is exemplary of our Foreign Affairs Committee, and that we are able to do things. I would remind Mr. Meeks and other members that we will be trying to put together a sense of the House resolution expressing concerns over the trends in Turkey, not condemnations but expressing concerns over the trends in Turkey.

When we are analyzing Turkey within the context of what is going on in the bigger picture and the EU is falling apart, think about this. Britain's exit of the EU, this is a first huge step—as huge, as someone else would say who may end up President—and so so we have got some changes.

And of course in our lifetime Turkey was constantly trying to become part of the EU and part of the common market. And now I think that is probably history. And I think that Erdogan represents more of a nationalistic Turkey focus rather than Europe focus approach. So these are all major changes that are going on. And let us hope that as these changes happen I believe that NATO—if we have a new President, if it is Mr. Trump, I would expect that NATO and the EU alliances would become less important and that individual deals and relationships between countries, respecting that each country has its own interest at stake, but trying to find the common ground where people can act together, that will replace some of the more systematized approaches that we have had since the beginning of the cold war and the cold war is over.

So with that said, whatever emerges in this new era, Turkey will play a very significant role. It is right there in the middle of everything.

So we have taken very seriously, we respect the people there. We are concerned that its trendline—and by the way just one last note, it has been my experience that whenever the suppression of the press goes up, the level of corruption rises at the same rate.

And if we have the suppression of various political elements in society, in Turkey. And we have the suppression of freedom of the press you can expect that there will be corruption as a result and it will not bode well for the people of Turkey. We are on their side.

And I now hold this committee adjourned.

53

[Whereupon, at 4:32 p.m., the subcommittee was adjourned.]

APPENDIX

SUBCOMMITTEE HEARING NOTICE
COMMITTEE ON FOREIGN AFFAIRS
U.S. HOUSE OF REPRESENTATIVES
WASHINGTON, DC 20515-6128

Subcommittee on Europe, Eurasia, and Emerging Threats (R-CA), Chairman

July 6, 2016

TO: MEMBERS OF THE COMMITTEE ON FOREIGN AFFAIRS

You are respectfully requested to attend an OPEN hearing of the Committee on Foreign Affairs, to be held by the Subcommittee on Europe, Eurasia, and Emerging Threats in Room 2172 of the Rayburn House Office Building (and available live on the Committee website at http://www.ForeignAffairs.house.gov):

DATE: Wednesday, July 13, 2016

TIME: 2:00 p.m.

SUBJECT: Turkey's Democratic Decline

WITNESS: Henri J. Barkey, Ph.D
                  Director
                  Middle East Program
                  Wilson Center

                  Fevzi Bilgin, Ph.D.
                  President
                  Rethink Institute

                  Mr. Alan Makovsky
                  Senior Fellow
                  Center for American Progress

By Direction of the Chairman

The Committee on Foreign Affairs seeks to make its facilities accessible to persons with disabilities. If you are in need of special accommodations, please call 202/225-5021 at least four business days in advance of the event, whenever practicable. Questions with regard to special accommodations in general (including availability of Committee materials in alternative formats and assistive listening devices) may be directed to the Committee.

COMMITTEE ON FOREIGN AFFAIRS

MINUTES OF SUBCOMMITTEE ON _____ *Europe, Eurasia, and Emerging Threats* _____ HEARING

Day__ *Wednesday*__ Date_____ *July 13, 2016*_____ Room___ **2200 RHOB**___

Starting Time _____ *2:54 pm*_____ Ending Time ___ *4:32 pm*___

Recesses | _0_ | (___to___)(___to___)(___to___)(___to___)(___to___)(___to___)

Presiding Member(s)

Rep. Rohrabacher

Check all of the following that apply:

Open Session ☑   Electronically Recorded (taped) ☑
Executive (closed) Session ☐   Stenographic Record ☑
Televised ☐

TITLE OF HEARING:

Turkey's Democratic Decline

SUBCOMMITTEE MEMBERS PRESENT:

Rep. Gabbard, Rep. Meeks, Rep. Trott, Rep. Weber

NON-SUBCOMMITTEE MEMBERS PRESENT: *(Mark with an * if they are not members of full committee.)*

N/A

HEARING WITNESSES: Same as meeting notice attached? Yes ☑ No ☐
(If "no", please list below and include title, agency, department, or organization.)

STATEMENTS FOR THE RECORD: *(List any statements submitted for the record.)*

1 Statement from Nina Ognianova (was orignially going to be a witness).

TIME SCHEDULED TO RECONVENE _____
or
TIME ADJOURNED ___ *4:32 pm*___

Subcommittee Staff Director

MATERIAL SUBMITTED FOR THE RECORD BY THE HONORABLE DANA ROHRABACHER, A REPRESENTATIVE IN CONGRESS FROM THE STATE OF CALIFORNIA, AND CHAIRMAN, SUBCOMMITTEE ON EUROPE, EURASIA, AND EMERGING THREATS

Testimony before the House Foreign Affairs Committee's
Europe, Eurasia, and Emerging Threats Subcommittee

Submitted by Nina Ognianova
Europe and Central Asia Program Coordinator
Committee to Protect Journalists

"Turkey's Democratic Decline"
Wednesday, July 13, 2016

Chairman Rohrabacher, Ranking Member Meeks, and members of the subcommittee:

Thank you for the opportunity to submit a written testimony at this hearing on human rights, democracy, and freedom of expression in Turkey. In my role as Europe and Central Asia program coordinator of the Committee to Protect Journalists (CPJ), an independent, nonprofit organization dedicated to defending press freedom and the rights of journalists worldwide, I have been focusing on Turkey since 2012. Along with my team, I have monitored and documented the government's crackdown on the media over the past four years, which has reached an unprecedented intensity.

In this testimony, I will focus on key methods the Turkish authorities have used to suppress opposition and independent media, and will highlight cases that illustrate the practice of these methods. I will offer recommendations to U.S. leaders on how they can support Turkish journalists and media outlets. Unless otherwise specified, all data cited in this testimony is based on CPJ research.

INTRODUCTION

For two consecutive years—2012 and 2013—Turkey was the leading jailer of journalists in the world, imprisoning more members of the press than repressive states such as Iran, China, and Eritrea. Over the next two years, due to both international advocacy and internal political processes, Turkey's record improved and it released dozens of journalists. However, at the same time the government increased its repressive action against the press, through using vague, broadly worded anti-terror laws; bringing charges under an archaic law that carries jail terms for insulting the president; replacing the editorial management of opposition media outlets and firing their staff; routinely imposing bans on the reporting of sensitive stories; and prosecuting and imprisoning journalists on anti-state charges in retaliation for their work.

Because of the high volume of attacks on the press taking place in Turkey, CPJ in March started publishing the Turkey Crackdown Chronicle: a daily summary of press freedom violations in the country. The chronicle, written and researched by CPJ's Turkey representative, can be found here. I urge you to follow it for current information on press freedom conditions in Turkey.

KEY PRESS FREEDOM ISSUES

IMPRISONMENT OF JOURNALISTS

Despite the release of multiple journalists in 2014—from a high of 61 in October 2012 to a low of seven in December 2014, Turkey continues to jail journalists for their work, and has increased the number of those detained and prosecuted on terrorism, propaganda, and anti-state charges in recent months. Turkey has targeted journalists with pro-Kurdish media outlets, including the daily *Özgür Gündem* and the Dicle News Agency (DIHA), for their coverage of clashes between Turkish security forces and Kurdish separatists in the southeast provinces, which have renewed since the collapse of fragile peace talks in 2015.

For months, Turkey imposed curfews that prevented the movement of civilians, including journalists, in and out of neighborhoods and towns in the south. Cities and districts, including the provincial center of Şırnak and the Sur district of Diyarbakir, remain under curfew today.

In one incident in the southeastern town of Cizre—which had been under a government-imposed curfew from early December 2015 until late February 2016, Rohat Aktaş, a news editor for the Kurdish-language daily *Azadiya Welat*, died in unclear circumstances. Aktaş had been trapped in a basement, where he sought shelter with others after being wounded in January. Aktaş, who was covering clashes, had reported getting injured in late January, 2016, before losing contact with his newsroom in early February, 2016. His charred body was recovered from the basement, after Turkish security forces apparently stormed the building which, according to authorities, was a hideout for militant separatists. According to the newsroom, Aktaş was not a fighter and was there only to report on the standoff between government forces and separatists. Turkish pro-government media said that the people trapped in the city were terrorists and that separatists had prevented ambulances from helping the injured. Pro-opposition and pro-Kurdish media reported that government forces were shooting indiscriminately at civilians and denying medical treatment to the injured. Because of the severe restrictions imposed on journalists, there were no independent accounts available to confirm the events.

The restrictions Turkish authorities have imposed on covering the south, as well as the region's volatility and distance from the media hubs of Istanbul and Ankara, make it hard to confirm the exact number of journalists detained in relation to their reporting, which is further complicated by the authorities' well-documented policy of using prison as a revolving door for members of the press. According to CPJ's ongoing documentation of imprisoned cases, Turkey currently holds at least 20 journalists in prison for their work.

PROSECUTION OF JOURNALISTS ON ANTI-STATE CHARGES

Using Turkey's vaguely worded anti-terrorism statutes, authorities routinely equate covering sensitive issues, such as the activities of the country's intelligence agency, the Kurdish issue, or the banned Kurdish Workers' Party (PKK), with terrorism. In one of the most high-profile cases that illustrates this trend, an Istanbul court in May convicted prominent investigative journalist Can Dündar of revealing state secrets, and sentenced him to seven years in prison (later reduced to five years and 10 months). He was first imprisoned, along with his colleague Erdem Gül, in November 2015 after a report in the independent daily *Cumhuriyet*—which Dündar edits—that alleged Turkish Intelligence Agency sent weapons to Syrian opposition groups. President Recep Tayyip Erdoğan publicly berated Dündar as a traitor before the journalist was jailed. International outcry, including statements by U.S. government officials, helped pressure authorities to release him from prison pending a trial. When the trial was held, it was closed to the public, President Erdoğan and the Turkish Intelligence Agency were admitted as formal complainants in the case, and Dündar and Gül were sentenced to jail. On the day of the verdict, an assailant shot at Dündar when he was talking to journalists during a break in proceedings. Dündar was unharmed, but a television journalist suffered injuries from a stray bullet.

The country's anti-state statutes are also used to prosecute media outlets. In an emblematic case, the pro-Kurdish daily *Özgür Gündem* and its staff are defendants in 149 individual trials for allegedly violating the vague Anti-Terrorism Law, as well as 27 trials for violating article 301 of the Turkish Penal Code, which makes it a crime to insult Turkey, the Turkish nation, or the Turkish state, according to the paper's lawyers.

Most recently, Erol Önderoğlu, Turkey representative for the press freedom group Reporters Without Borders, was jailed alongside another journalist, and a human rights activist on terrorism propaganda charges after they took part in a campaign of solidarity with *Özgür Gündem*, in which local journalists served as rotating editors at the newspaper. Önderoğlu and his fellow campaigners were freed pending trial after international groups made multiple calls for their release.

In June 2016, Ankara prosecutors opened criminal investigations under the Anti-Terror Law against eight television stations and two daily newspapers on suspicion of spreading propaganda for the PKK, which Turkey classifies as a terrorist group. According to local news reports, prosecutors from the Office of Crimes Against the Constitution are investigating broadcasters İMC TV, Hayat TV, MED NUÇE TV, STREK TV, K24, VAN TV, RONAHİ TV, NEWROZ TV and the daily newspapers *Evrensel* and *Özgür Gündem* on the accusation. Three months earlier, Turkey's largest signal provider, Türksat Satellite Communication and Cable TV Operation, dropped İMC TV's signal permanently, acting on order of the Ankara Public Prosecutor's Office, on similar accusations. İMC TV found an alternative signal provider with smaller coverage, but continued to face government persecution.

INSULTING THE PRESIDENT

Since his inauguration in August 2014, President Erdoğan has used Article 299 of Turkey's penal code, "Insulting the President," more than any of his predecessors. The law, which dates back to 1926, carries a prison term of more than four years if the content deemed to be offensive is published in the press. In the first seven months of Erdoğan's presidency, 236 people were investigated under the law, with 105 indicted, according to a BBC report that cited statistics from Turkey's Justice Ministry. The defendants have included journalists as well as students, civil activists, scholars, artists, and even a former Miss Turkey. By March 2016, according to Justice Minister Bekir Bozdağ, 1,845 cases were pending. The cases against journalists have been levied in connection to articles, broadcasts, books, social media posts, and comments in Internet chat forums. In the case of at least one journalist, his defense in court resulted in insult charges. Barış İnce, editor-in-chief of the leftist daily *BirGün*, had written a defense in October 2014 (in a separate defamation case against him), using an acrostic—in which the first letter of each line spells out a phrase—that included the words "Thief Tayyip," a common chant of anti-government protesters. The defense was delivered in court and was printed in *BirGün*. On March 8, 2016, an Istanbul court convicted İnce of insulting the president and sentenced him to 21 months in prison. His appeal is still pending.

GOVERNMENT TAKEOVERS OF OPPOSITION OUTLETS

In October 2015, Istanbul police broke the gates of the Koza İpek Group building in Istanbul's Şişli district and used water cannons and tear gas against protesters who had gathered in support of the five news outlets including the television stations, Bugün TV and Kanaltürk TV, belonging to the company. Police stormed the premises and shut down live television broadcasts two days after a Turkish court ordered the management of the privately owned company to be replaced with government-friendly trustees. The broadcasts of Bugün TV and Kanaltürk TV, which were cut during the raid, and which had provided political debate and opposition views in the run-up to November 1, 2015, parliamentary elections, were replaced with documentaries on World War II and the lives of camels. Bugün TV, Kanaltürk TV, as well as Kanaltürk radio, and the daily newspapers *Bugün* and *Millet,* were all eventually shut down, according to press reports.

In a similar move, in March 2016, an Istanbul court ordered that the managerial and editorial boards of news outlets belonging to the Feza Media Group be taken over by government-appointed trustees. Riot police stormed the premises of Turkey's largest-circulation newspaper, *Zaman,* and its sister-publication, the English-language daily *Today's Zaman.* Journalists were fired and several were forced into exile for fear of politically motivated prosecution. Overnight, *Zaman*—previously a staunch government critic—printed an issue favorable to President Erdoğan and his policies. The new government-appointed managers took over servers belonging to *Zaman* and *Today's Zaman,* and blocked journalists' from accessing the newspapers' websites. The publications' digital archives were deleted, according to press reports and CPJ contacts at both newspapers.

The repressive actions against the Koza İpek Group and the Feza Media Group are part of a wider crackdown by Turkey on media associated with the Gülenist movement—followers of exiled preacher Fethullah Gülen, an ally-turned-critic of the ruling Justice and Development Party, whom the government accuses of maintaining a terrorist organization and a "parallel state structure" within Turkey. The allegations have not been substantiated.

In early June 2016, Ankara prosecutors opened a criminal investigation against the small television station Can Erzincan TV on accusations of producing propaganda for the Gülenist movement under the country's Anti-Terror Law. The station was started shortly after the takeover of the Koza İpek Group by journalists formally employed by the group.

NEWS BLACKOUTS, BLOCKING WEBSITES

It is standard practice in Turkey to impose news bans on sensitive stories, including terrorist attacks, and natural and man-made disasters. Regulators frequently censor social media websites following attacks, though many Turkish internet users are able to circumvent the censorship.

Following deadly blasts at Istanbul's Atatürk airport on June 28, 2016, regulators issued a partial ban on coverage. Regulators temporarily blocked access to the social media websites Facebook, Twitter, and YouTube, according to *Turkish Minute,* an English-language opposition news website. Internet freedom activists published a statement from the Information and Communications Technologies Authority

(BTK) shortly after the attacks, warning Turkish social media users that sharing security camera footage of the bombings—including those who "retweet" or "repost" such videos—could face legal action. In the statement, the BTK warned social media users against "serving the means of terrorism."

Also in June, the state broadcast regulator RTÜK fined the left-leaning Hayatın Sesi TV channel for violating a partial ban on coverage of a March 19, 2016 bomb attack in Istanbul, and for interviews it aired on March 24 with residents of Cizre, the site of fighting between Kurdish separatists and security forces. RTÜK issued a warning to Hayatın Sesi TV over its coverage of the bomb attack, and fined it 14,350 Turkish liras (US$4,886) for the interviews with residents. If regulators find the station has violated its rules a third time within the year, they can ban the station from broadcasting for 10 days. A fourth violation in a year could result in the station losing its license, the left-leaning daily *Evrensel* reported.

While news bans are enforceable at broadcast media, they do little to stem the information flow online. To censor reporting on the internet, the government resorts to blocking entire websites. In a recent case documented by CPJ, on July 1 2016 Turkey's telecommunications regular, the TİB, blocked access to four websites deemed sympathetic to the Gülenist movement. The website of the newspaper *Yeni Hayat* was blocked because of a story it ran after the June 28 Istanbul attacks, which alleged there could be as many as 150 suicide bombers in Turkey. The website of the daily *Yarına Bakış* and the news websites *Subohaber* and *Onyediyirmibes*, whose coverage is also sympathetic to the Gülenist movement, reported on social media that regulators had blocked them without explanation.

Turkish authorities aggressively attempt to censor social media, particularly Twitter. The platform has become a viable alternative source of information and commentary to traditional media, which are largely under government control. According to the latest transparency report by Twitter, in the months July-December 2015, the company received 2,211 removal of information requests from Turkey, more than from any other country in the world.

RECOMMENDATIONS

Despite Turkey's seeming defiance to international criticism of its human rights and press freedom record, the government does take notice of U.S. leaders' public statements and actions of support, and is in turn moved to act on them. According to multiple CPJ sources in Turkey, Washington currently has more leverage on Ankara than any other capital in the world. The U.S. must use this leverage to speak publicly and unequivocally in support of both individual cases and press freedom principles in Turkey, and it must use every opportunity to condition diplomatic, economic, and strategic benefits by the U.S. for Turkey on tangible, meaningful press freedom and freedom of expression improvements by Ankara. Specifically, U.S. leaders must demand that Turkey release all journalists imprisoned in retaliation for their work; reform its anti-terror laws to exclude all anti-press statutes; scrap Article 299 of the penal code that criminalizes insulting the president; cease the practice of prosecuting journalists on anti-state charges; stop censoring the media, including through blocking online speech and news bans; return all seized opposition media outlets to their rightful owners and managers; and lift all restrictions to independent reporting on, and from, Turkey's volatile southeast regions.

Thank you for providing CPJ with the opportunity to address this important matter.